PRAISE FOR *BONE BLACK*

"*Bone Black* is a lucid, challenging and entrancing read."
—*The Washington Post Book World*

"hooks has fashioned a hypnotic, faintly otherworldly memoir that is at once familiar and unique."
—*The Boston Globe*

"bell hooks's *Bone Black* is a lively, lyrical memoir."
—*Elle* magazine

"hooks's recollection of family, race, religion, sex, class, and gender . . . linger long after being absorbed into your mind. . . . *Bone Black* is hooks at her most personal and passionately honest; it's one of her best yet."
—*Vibe* magazine

"*Bone Black* . . . is a canvas of vividly impressionistic splashes of growing up young, gifted, black, and female."
—*The Philadelphia Inquirer*

"bell hooks's memoir is flat out remarkable. . . . The two most striking things about *Bone Black* are hooks's seductively simple prose style, and the way she tackles everything from integration, to sexuality, to love of books with a mixture of straightforwardness and sensitivity."
—*Capital Times*

"Reading hooks's memoir is a warm and rewarding experience that challenges the unspoken value system that molds the self-image of many black women."

—*American Statesman*

"It is a most soul-searching and tender work."

—*The Black Collegian*

"hooks's exquisite prose, forged in the heat of inner fires, glows like obsidian."

—*Booklist*

Previous books by bell hooks

BONE BLACK

Bone Black

memories of girlhood

—————

bell hooks

An Owl Book

Henry Holt and Company / New York

Henry Holt and Company, Inc.
Publishers since 1866
115 West 18th Street
New York, New York 10011

Henry Holt ® is a registered trademark of
Henry Holt and Company, Inc.

Library of Congress Cataloging-in-Publication Data
hooks, bell.
Bone Black: memories of girlhood / bell hooks.
p.   cm.
1. hooks, bell—Childhood and youth. 2. Afro-Americans—Biography.
3. Afro-American women—Biography. 4. Feminists—United States
Biography. I. Title.
E185.97.H77A3 1996   96-7308
[B]305.48896'073—dc20   CIP

ISBN 0-8050-5512-6

Henry Holt books are available for special promotions and
premiums. For details contact: Director, Special Markets.

First published in hardcover in 1996 by
Henry Holt and Company, Inc.

First Owl Book Edition—1996

Designed by Michelle McMillian

Printed in the United States of America
All first editions are printed on acid-free paper. ∞

5 7 9 10 8 6 4

to my best "girl"
with hope for the boy I held in my arms.

when you say "I would die for you" to those you love,
the truth of those words may be not that you give your
physical life but that you are willing to die to the past
and be born again in the present where you can live fully
and freely—where you can give us the love we need.

Foreword

Bone Black: memories of girlhood is not an ordinary tale. It is the story of girlhood rebellion, of my struggle to create self and identity distinct from and yet inclusive of the world around me. Writing imagistically, I seek to conjure a rich magical world of southern black culture that was sometimes paradisical and at others times terrifying. While the narratives of family life I share can be easily labeled dysfunctional, significantly that fact will never alter the magic and mystery that was present—all that was deeply life sustaining and life affirming. The beauty lies in the way it all comes together exposing and revealing the inner life of a girl inventing herself—creating the foundation of self-hood and identity that will ultimately lead to the fulfillment of her true destiny—becoming a writer.

Nowadays, more than ever before, feminist thinkers are

writing about the significance of girlhood as a time when females feel free and powerful. Our bodies do not yet distinguish themselves as definitively from those of boys. And our energies are just as intense if not more so. Not enough is known about the experience of black girls in our society. Indeed, one of my favorite novels in the whole world is Toni Morrison's *The Bluest Eye*. When the book was first published she explained that it was her desire to write about "the people who in all literature were always peripheral—little black girls who were props, background; those people were never center stage and those people were me." I was still in my teens when I read this book. It shook me to the very roots of my being. There in this fictional narrative were fragments of my story—my girlhood. Always an obsessive reader, I had felt this lack. To see this period of our life given serious recognition was awesomely affirming. My life was never going to be the same after reading this book. It wasn't simply that Morrison focused on black girls but that she gave us girls confronting issues of class, race, identity, girls who were struggling to confront and cope with pain. And most of all she gave us black girls who were critical thinkers, theorizing their lives, telling the story, and by so doing making themselves subjects of history.

Many feminist thinkers writing and talking about girlhood right now like to suggest that black girls have better self-esteem than their white counterparts. The measurement of this difference is often that black girls are more assertive, speak more, appear more confident. Yet in traditional southern-based black life, it was and is expected of girls to be articulate, to hold ourselves with dignity. Our parents and teachers were always urging us to stand up right and speak clearly. These traits were meant to uplift the race. They were not necessarily traits associated with building female self-esteem. An outspoken girl might still feel that she was worthless because her skin was not light enough or her hair the right texture. These are the variables that white researchers often do not consider when they measure the self-esteem of black females with a yardstick that was designed based on values emerging from white experience. White girls of all classes are often encouraged to be silent. But to see the opposite in different ethnic groups as a sign of female empowerment is to miss the reality that the cultural codes of that group may dictate a quite different standard by which female self-esteem is measured. To understand the complexity of black girlhood we need more work that documents that reality in all its variations and diversity. Certainly, class shapes the nature of our childhood experiences. Undoubtedly, black girls raised in materially privileged families have different notions of self-esteem from peers growing up poor and/or destitute. It's vital then that we hear about our diverse experience. There is no one story of black girlhood.

As a girl growing up in a family that includes five sisters, I am amazed that our experiences were often incredibly different even though we were in the same household. Our memories reflect those differences. *Bone Black: memories of girlhood* is my story. An unconventional memoir, it draws together the experiences, dreams, and fantasies that most preoccupied me as a girl. I share my secret world—the various names I created, for example (calling my grandmother Saru in my imagination because it was better than her real name, Sarah). This is autobiography as truth and myth—as poetic witness. That rebellious writer of the Beat generation Jack Kerouac always declared "memories are inseparable from dreams." In *Bone Black* I gather together the dreams, fantasies, experiences that preoccupied me as a girl, that stay with me and appear and reappear in different shapes and forms in all my work. Without telling everything that happened, they document all that remains most vivid. They are the foundation on which I have built a life in writing, a life committed to intellectual pursuits.

Laying out the groundwork of my early life like a crazy quilt, *Bone Black* brings together fragments to make a whole. Bits and pieces connect in a random and playfully irrational way. And there is always the persistence of repetition, for that is what the mind does—goes over and over the same things looking at them in different ways. The prevailing perspective is always that of the intuitive and critically thinking child mind. Sometimes memories are presented in the third person, indirectly, just as all of us sometimes talk about things that way. We look back as if we are standing at a distance. Examining life retrospectively we are there and not there, watching and watched. Evoking the mood and sensibility of moments, this is an autobiography of perceptions and ideas. The events described are always less significant than the impressions they leave on the mind and heart.

The child I was has been left behind.
Those who first loved me have gone on without me.
Where they were a door has been left open upon a solitude.
—Robert Duncan, *Ground Work*

Our lives may be determined less by our childhood than
by the way we have learned to imagine our childhoods.
—James Hillman, *The Soul's Code*

BONE BLACK

memories of girlhood

1

MAMA HAS GIVEN me a quilt from her hope chest. It is one her mother's mother made. It is a quilt of stars—each piece taken from faded-cotton summer dresses—each piece stitched by hand. She has given me a beaded purse that belonged to my father's mother Sister Ray. They want to know why she has given it to me since I was not Sister Ray's favorite. They say she is probably turning over in her grave angry that I have something of hers.

Mama tells us—her daughters—that the girls in her family started gathering things for their hope chest when they were very young, gathering all the things that they would carry with them into marriage. The first time she opens hers for us I feel I am witnessing yet another opening of Pandora's box, that the secrets of her youth, the bittersweet memories, will come rushing out like a waterfall and push us back in time. Instead the scent of cedar fills the air. It reminds me of Christmas, of abandoned trees, standing naked in the snow after the celebrations are over. Usually we are not invited to share in the opening of the chest. Even though we stand near her watching, she acts as if we are not there. I see her remembering, clutching tightly in her hand some object, some bit of herself that she has had to part with in order to live in the present. I see her examining each hope to see if it has been fulfilled, if the promises have been kept. I pretend I do not see the tears in her eyes. I am glad she shares the opening of the chest this time with all of us. I am clutching the gifts she hands to me, the quilt, the beaded purse. She knows that I am often hopeless. She stores no treasures for my coming marriage. I do not want to be given away. I cannot contain my dreams until tomorrow. I cannot wait for someone else, a stranger, to take my hand.

That night in my sleep I dream of going away. I am taking the bus. Mama is standing waving good-bye. Later when I return from my journey I come home only to find there has been a fire, nothing remains of our house and I can see no one. There is only the dark and the thick smell of smoke. I stand alone weeping. The sound of my sobbing is like the cry of the peacock. Suddenly they appear with candles, mama and everyone. They say they have heard my sorrow pierce the air like the cry of the peacock, that they have come to comfort me. They give me a candle. Together we search the ashes for bits and pieces, any fragment of our lives that may have survived. We find that the hope chest has not burned through and through. We open it, taking out the charred remains. Someone finds a photo, one face has turned to ash, another is there. We pass around the fragments like bread and wine at communion. The chorus of weeping is our testimony that we are moved.

Louder than our weeping is a voice commanding us to stop our tears. We cannot see who is speaking but we are reminded of the stern sound of our mother's mother's voice. We listen. She tells us to sit close in the night, to make a circle of our bodies, to place the candles at the center of the circle. The candles burn like another fire only this time she says the fire burns to warm our hearts. She says Listen, let me tell you a story. She begins to put together in words all that has been destroyed in the fire. We are all rejoicing when the dream ends.

The next day I want to know what the dream means, who she is, this storyteller who comes in the night. Saru, mama's mother, is the interpreter of dreams. She tells me that I should know the storyteller, that I and she are one, that they are my sisters, family. She says that a part of me is making the story, making the words, making the new fire, that it is my heart burning in the center of the flames.

2

WE LIVE IN the country. We children do not understand that that means we are among the poor. We do not understand that the outhouses behind many of the houses are still there because running water came here long after they had it in the city. We do not understand that our playmates who are eating laundry starch do so not because the white powder tastes so good but because they are sometimes without necessary food. We do not understand that we wash with the heavy, unsmelling, oddly shaped pieces of homemade lye soap because real soap costs money. We never think about where lye soap comes from. We only know we want to make our skin itch less—that we do not want our mouths to be washed out with it. Because we are poor, because we live in the country, we go to the country school—the little white wood-frame building where all the country kids come. They come from miles and miles away. They come so far because they are black. As they are riding the school buses they pass school after school where children who are white can attend without being bused, without getting up in the wee hours of the morning, sometimes leaving home in the dark.

We are not bused. The school is only a mile or two away from our house. We get to walk. We get to wander aimlessly in the road—until a car comes by. We get to wave at the buses. They are not allowed to stop and give us a ride. We do not understand why. Daddy says the walk to school will be good for us. He tells us again and again in a harsh voice of the miles he walked to school through fields in the snow, without boots or gloves to keep him warm. We are not comforted by the image of the small boy trudging along many miles to school so he can learn to read and be somebody. When we close our eyes he becomes real to us. He looks very sad. Sometimes he cries. We are not at all comforted. And there are still days when we complain about the walk, especially when it is wet and stormy.

School begins with chapel. There we recite the Pledge of Allegiance to the Flag. We have no feeling for the flag but we like the words; said in unison, they sound like a chant. We then listen to a morning prayer. We say the Lord's Prayer. It is the singing that makes morning chapel the happiest moment of the day. It is there I learn to sing "Red River Valley." It is a song about missing and longing. I do not understand all the words, only the feeling—warm wet sorrow, like playing games in spring rain. After chapel we go to classrooms.

In the first grade the teacher gives tasting parties. She brings us different foods to taste so that we can know what they are like because we do not eat them in our homes. All of us eagerly await the Fridays when the tasting part will begin. The day she brings cottage cheese I am not sure I want to try it. She makes me. She makes everyone try a little bit just in case they might really like it. We go home from the tasting parties telling our parents what it was like, telling them to buy this new good food, better food, better than any food we have ever tasted.

Mama tells us that most of that food we taste isn't good to eat all the time, that it is a waste of money. We do not understand money. We do not know that we are all poor. We cannot visit many of the friends we make because they live miles and miles away. We have each other after school.

3

HERE AT THE country school we must always work to raise money—selling candy, raffle tickets, having shows for which tickets are sold. Sold to our parents, neighbors, friends, people without money who are shamed into buying little colored paper they cannot afford, tickets that will help keep the school going. The people with lots of money can buy many tickets—can show that they are "big time." Their flesh is often the color of pigs in the storybook. Somehow they have more money because they are lighter, because their flesh turns pink and pinker, because they dye their hair blond, red, to emphasize the light, lightness of their skin. We children think of them as white. We are so confused by this thing called Race.

We learn about color with crayons. We learn to tell the difference between white and pink and a color they call

Flesh. The flesh-colored crayon amuses us. Like white it never shows up on the thick Manila paper they give us to draw on, or on the brown paper sacks we draw on at home. Flesh we know has no relationship to our skin, for we are brown and brown and brown like all good things. And we know that pigs are not pink or white like these flesh people. We secretly love pigs, especially me. I like to watch them lie in the mud, covering themselves in the cool red mud that is like clay, that is flaming red hot like dirt on fire. I like to watch them eat—to feed them. For some weeks now I have been feeding them the coal that is our way of keeping warm in winters. I give them little pieces at a time to hear the crunching sound. I want to give them all the tickets to eat so no one will have to sell them, so mama will not have to complain about the way it adds to her worries that she must now sell tickets. The pigs are disgusted by the tickets. Even when I prod them with a stick they only turn away. They would rather eat coal.

I must sell tickets for a Tom Thumb wedding, one of the school shows. It isn't any fun for children. We get to dress up in paper wedding clothes and go through a ceremony for the entertainment of the adults. The whole thing makes me sick but no one cares. Like every other girl I want to be the bride but I am not chosen. It has always to do with money. The important roles go to the children whose parents have money to give, who will work hard selling tickets. I am lucky to be a bridesmaid, to wear a red crepe paper dress made just for me. I am not thrilled with such luck. I would rather not wear a paper dress, not be in a make-believe wedding. They tell me that I am lucky to be lighter skinned, not black black, not dark brown, lucky to have hair that is almost straight, otherwise I might not be in the wedding at all, otherwise I might not be so lucky.

This luck angers me and when I am angry things always go wrong. We are practicing in our paper dresses, walking down the aisle while the piano music plays a wedding march. We are practicing to be brides, to be girls who will grow up to be given away. My legs would rather be running, itch to go outdoors. My legs are dreaming, adventurous legs. They cannot walk down the aisle without protest. They go too fast. They go too slow. They make everything slow down. The girl walking behind me steps on the red dress; it tears. It moves from my flesh like wind moving against the running legs. I am truly lucky now to have this tear. I hope they will make me sit, but they say No we would not think of taking you out of the show. They know how much every girl wants to be in a wedding. The tear must be mended. The red dress like a woman's heart must break silently and in secret.

4

WHERE THEY LIVE on the hill there are few houses around. All the land is owned by one black man who lives not far away from them in a big house with no other houses around. He also lives high on a hill. Their house is made of stone and concrete. White men built it when they began work to see if oil could be found on the hill. Oil was never found. They left remnants of their machinery, of their presence. They left the cold concrete house. In the hot humid summer the coolness inside was like refrigeration but in the winter it was cold and damp. The cold grayness of the house had little impact on them. They were always playing outside, playing in the green grasses and hills above the house. They would walk for miles into the hills looking for honeysuckle and wild asparagus, trying to stay out of the way of snakes. They were not always afraid of snakes but they knew to be careful, knew that snakebite could be dangerous.

She liked to walk to a favorite tree up the hill and play with a bright green snake that lived there, a green tree snake. She knew how to talk to the snake and how to listen. She told the snake about the problems she was having learning her left from her right. The snake understood her frustration, her tears, when everyone was ready to go and she was still struggling to put her shoes on the correct foot. The snake understood that the punishments did not make the task any easier. She felt it was the shoes. Big Buster Brown shoes that she and her brother wore. Wrapped around her wrist like a bracelet, the green tree snake told her to take those shoes every day and put them on the trash, that maybe they would burn them along with all unwanted things. Every night she sneaked out of the house and placed the shoes neatly on the pile of trash to be burned. Every morning she was punished and made to get the shoes. She continued until finally her daddy said Buy her another pair of shoes. She was considered a problem child, a child intent on getting her own way. That day she wandered off alone to thank the green tree snake for helping her. On her way home she found a new path. Without thinking she followed it. The path led to a huge garden. She did not know who had planted it. She walked slowly down row after row, watching the growing plants, making sure not to step on them. Walking down the rows made her dizzy maybe that was why she stumbled and fell, scraping both knees on the gravel and dirt as she rolled a bit down the hill. She lay crying, lost and alone. The some-one who picked her up was a man she did not know. He was not an old man. His skin was pink like the pig's skin. His hair was black and curly. When he picked her up he told her he was carrying her home. She was sure the snake had sent him. She told him all about the snake—how it was her one true friend. He laughed, asking her if he could be her friend. She was sure about snakes not about strange men so she said nothing. He carried her all the way home. They had been searching the hills for her calling her name.

At home the man introduced himself as the landlord's son. Before he left he promised to marry her, to come back when she was older. The grown-ups seemed to think this was a good idea. She whispered a secret in his ear. She told him that she could not marry him because she had already promised the snake that they could live together forever near their favorite tree.

5

HE HAD AN old car. It was never moved. It sunk in the mud as if it had grown up from it like any other plant. Only it was clearly not a plant—it was in every sense of the word a man-made creature. Their hands would caress the deep red leather like silk against the skin. They knew it was flesh—knew it could sense the awe in their touch. They played games inside the car. It was a favorite hiding place. Crouching uncomfortably on the floor like a terrified animal, they would dream about what it would be like to never be found—but they were always found.

She particularly liked hiding in the car, locking all the doors so no one could get inside. She liked grinning through the glass at the face of grown-ups as they pleaded with her to open the door. She liked watching their terror. She sometimes felt terror.

Once her mother was in the hospital and Sister Ray, her father's mother, came to take care of them. They never understood why anyone needed to take care of them. Deep down inside they were afraid that this anonymous someone was coming to take their mother's place; they did not want another caretaker, they wanted only mama. Because she was not Sister Ray's favorite she dreaded her coming. She came anyway, with her stern face the color of shiny bright coal, the color of darkness, the face she had given to her son. It was whispered that she did not care for this particular little one because her face was not even thinking about being brown enough, was not even changing in the sun. This particular little one heard the whispers. She bitterly resented this hatred. It was her first rejection. She wanted to hide from it, so naturally she chose the car. It was the safest hiding place—there one could be found and not found at the same time. Only this hiding she did not want to do alone—so they, her brother and sisters, joined her. At first they did not roll the windows up. They just locked all the doors. They waited for Sister Ray to discover that they were all gone—that the house was too quiet. When she finally sensed them missing and couldn't find them in the house—they could hear her calling.—she came outdoors searching. They quickly rolled the windows up and crouched on the seats, their hot young bodies touching one another as they laughed. It wasn't working. She did not think to look in the car. They rolled the windows down and called to her.

She stood still, staring at them for a minute as if she could not believe her eyes. They were so close and yet she had felt such fear. The corners of her mouth began to tighten, she looked at them cold and hard. It was the look that communicated the pain of punishment before the switches tied together would tear and burn their flesh. They looked at her and could feel the burning. They closed the windows tight, shutting off the little cracks they had wanted for air, the little cracks that enabled them to hear her ordering them to Get out this minute.

Defiant, determined, they refused to budge even though they were beginning to feel afraid. Their resolve was weakening. They knew that the longer they remained in the car, the more intense the punishment. They wanted to relent but the particular little one, the one who was not her favorite, couldn't resist a last rebellious display. She spit—right in the direction of that stern face. Only the rolled up window kept it from reaching the target. Shocked, they opened the doors and ran, leaving her sitting alone contemplating the coming punishment.

6

TERROR FASCINATED HER. She wanted to understand its ability to arouse. In her child mind it was always associated with cars. She decided then never to learn to drive. They were in the yard playing with a four-year-old. They had been warned about staying on the sidewalk, out of the street. No one ever thought that those words sidewalk, street, like the concrete they were both made of, merged into one big stretch for a four-year-old imagination. When she moved into the street it was as if it did not exist as a place where cars might come, she could not even hear them. It was a good thing then for the little girl that the car was not moving very fast, that the driver saw her and slowed down, that the other passenger called out. It was a good thing that the older children watching yelled her name, ran to grab her. Standing there holding the child's hand—the child who was not crying because all the moment's terror had communicated itself unspoken into every bit of her body—she recalled the terror she felt, the terror in the eyes of the driver, the passenger, momentarily flashing like lightning then gone. The scene replayed itself over and over—the sounds, the screech of brakes, the smell, the terror of the child, the terrorized parent spanking the child to communicate sidewalk, street, car, hurt. She was stunned.

They always went for drives. It was one way the family and mostly the mother could get out of the house and into the street. They would drive around visiting family, looking at neighborhoods. The slow movement of the car in summer heat always lulled her into a trancelike sleep—she forgot about its ability to arouse terror. Suddenly its stopping would remind her. At any moment the brakes could screech, the child living inside her could be run down.

They lived near the railroad tracks. Sitting in the hot car with the silent man and the woman trying ever so hard to please, they would count the number of cars in the train. They would imagine places the train would take them. They would sink into the sound of the whistle as if it echoed every promise of adventure and return. Trains were without terror. They could take you everywhere and bring you back, safe, in one piece, in one body. When the trains were coming red warning lights would flash; but they did not always work on the side of town where the poor and unwanted lived.

She could not remember if the lights were flashing that day. She remembered that they had begun to move across the tracks when the car came to a stop. They waited as the father tried to get the car going, listening to the sounds as he turned the key again and again, muttering words that explained nothing to the silent listeners who had already begun to feel worried, afraid. He got out to look under the hood, to find the problem, fix it. They sat there speechless and thirsty, fear drying their throats like sand on a desert. They sat there longing for circuses and vanilla ice cream, quiet only because they feared punishment. They feared that any moment the trains with all the cars they loved, with the bright red cabooses they took to be emblems of victory, would have no time to stop for an unmoving car. They and the car would be crushed. Whether she saw the train coming she was never able to say, only that she felt it, felt terror rising in her like a fierce tide washing away all remnants of loving observers. Mixed with the terror was a feeling of awe as she saw the father running for safety, saw him standing near the flashing red lights.

7

SHE WAS CLOSEST to her brother. Not only were they just months apart in age but they looked alike. They looked like twins even though he was older. Like twins they shared the same dreams and longings, the same devotion to one another. Strangely enough it was a toy that separated them, that forced upon them different roles, different identities. She remembered the toy—a bright red wagon. They shared possession of it but they had different roles in relationship to it. She was to ride in the red wagon and he was to pull it. She was to ride in it because she was a girl—a would-be princess whom some rich prince would come seeking, take away to his palace, and keep her there in splendor forever. He was to pull it because he was a boy—a would-be prince who would do all the hard work, slay the dragons, fight the slimy creatures, challenge the fat ugly men so that he could carry away the beautiful princess. He never carried her any further than the corner of the street and all the while he complained bitterly about how awful it was pulling her, how he wanted a turn sitting in the wagon. Sometimes he would cry—that was just how much he wanted to be pulled in the red wagon.

She did not mind pulling him. It was the grown-ups like Papa her great-grandfather who had trouble seeing her pull that big boy in the wagon. When they finally got daring enough to go around the corner he would immediately dump her out and demand that he be pulled. Her legs were short and fat, his were long. She could not pull as fast as he wanted her to but he urged her on, watching with glee as the little fat legs struggled to move him, fast, faster, struggled to give him the fastest ride of them all. Her struggle to give him the fast ride made the boy happy, so happy that he never wanted to take turns. He only wanted her to pull and pull him. It was because of this that she began to assert her girl rights, to tell him that he was the boy and should pull her. He rarely listened so she would threaten to tell the grown-ups. He would always say, Tell them, knowing all the time that she would not, that she hated to see him punished. If he was punished she would want to be punished, too; even if they would not punish her she would cry with him. Sometimes the father and the great-grandfather would find out that the boy rarely pulled the girl. They would stand towering over him speaking in harsh big voices, explaining that he was the boy and should do this, explaining to him that if he did not do what boys should do they would take the toy away, give it to the girl only, not let them share it. She was always standing in the background listening—waiting to hear the boy tell her when they were alone that he hate, hate, hated her because she was a girl.

She grew up not remembering why the red wagon had been so important. She grew up and found that the red wagon of her memory had never existed. Going through boxes of old black-and-white photos, she found many of herself plump and unsmiling seated in a wheelbarrow with the boy-brother holding the ends as if at any moment he would dump her out. In the photos the boy looks very happy and self-important. She looks apprehensive, unsure. Seeing that the toy of her memory was a wheelbarrow she understood why there had always been bruises, dirty torn clothes. She had never understood why she would have fallen out of a wagon, but a wheelbarrow she could understand. She could understand the boy's pleasure, his longing, his constant sorrow.

No one could tell her what happened to the red wheelbarrow. No one knew whether it was kept at the house of Papa the great-grandfather. They could not remember playing with it anywhere else. He lived on a side of town where there were sidewalks, maybe that is why they only played with it there, maybe it disappeared because of their constant fighting, because of the boy's whining, maybe he made it disappear.

8

WE LEARN EARLY that it is important for a woman to marry. We are always marrying our dolls to someone. He of course is always invisible, that is until they made the Ken doll to go with Barbie. One of us has been given a Barbie doll for Christmas. Her skin is not white white but almost brown from the tan they have painted on her. We know she is white because of her blond hair. The newest Barbie is bald, with many wigs of all different colors. We spend hours dressing and undressing her, pretending she is going somewhere important. We want to make new clothes for her. We want to buy the outfits made just for her that we see in the store but they are too expensive. Some of them cost as much as real clothes for real people. Barbie is anything but real, that is why we like her. She never does housework, washes dishes, or has children to care for. She is free to spend all day dreaming about the Kens of the world. Mama laughs when we tell her there should be more than one Ken for Barbie, there should be Joe, Sam, Charlie, men in all shapes and sizes. We do not think that Barbie should have a girlfriend. We know that Barbie was born to be alone—that the fantasy woman, the soap opera girl, the girl of *True Confessions,* the Miss America girl was born to be alone. We know that she is not us.

My favorite doll is brown, brown like light milk chocolate. She is a baby doll and I give her a baby doll name, Baby. She is almost the same size as a real baby. She comes with no clothes, only a pink diaper, fastened with tiny gold pins and a plastic bottle. She has a red mouth the color of lipstick slightly open so that we can stick the bottle in it. We fill the bottle with water and wait for it to come through the tiny hole in Baby's bottom. We make her many new diapers, but we are soon bored with changing them. We lose the bottle and Baby can no longer drink. We still love her. She is the only doll we will not destroy. We have lost Barbie. We have broken the leg of another doll. We have cracked open the head of an antique doll to see what makes the crying sound. The little thing inside is not interesting. We are sorry but nothing can be done— not even mama can put the pieces together again. She tells us that if this is the way we intend to treat our babies she hopes we do not have any. She laughs at our careless parenting. Sometimes she takes a minute to show us the right thing to do. She too is terribly fond of Baby. She says that she looks so much like a real newborn. Once she came up-stairs, saw Baby under the covers, and wanted to know who had brought the real baby from downstairs.

She loves to tell the story of how Baby was born. She tells us that I, her problem child, decided out of nowhere that I did not want a white doll to play with, I demanded a brown doll, one that would look like me. Only grown-ups think that the things children say come out of nowhere. We know they come from the deepest parts of ourselves. Deep within myself I had begun to worry that all this lov-ing care we gave to the pink and white flesh-colored dolls meant that somewhere left high on the shelves were boxes of unwanted, unloved brown dolls covered in dust. I thought that they would remain there forever, orphaned and alone, unless someone began to want them, to want to give them love and care, to want them more than anything. At first they ignored my wanting. They complained. They pointed out that white dolls were easier to find, cheaper. They never said where they found Baby but I know. She was always there high on the shelf, covered in dust—waiting.

9

BIG MAMA—TO us she is special, unique, one of a kind. We do not know that there are other big mamas in the world. She is short and fat. We stand and look straight into her eyes even though we are children. We know she is old because she is our father's mother's mother, because she does not read or write, because she chews tobacco and smokes a pipe. We know that women did those things in the old-old days. We like the pipe, the circles of smoke that form in the air. We like to take a puff now and then. We do not like the chewing tobacco. It means that we must find empty coffee cans and stuff them with newspaper so Big Mama can spit. We do not like these makeshift spittoons. She tells us that everyone had them once. She is the only one we know who uses them. As soon as she is done visiting we rush to throw them away. Short and fat, she walks with a cane to give herself support. We think her kindness and generosity are related to her fat. She never yells at us—never treats us harshly. The grown-ups say she lets us have our way. They are not eager to let us go and stay at her house. We come back spoiled.

We love her. We show our love by endlessly kissing and hugging her. She does not mind. She laughs when they yell at us to stay away, to get back. She wears aprons over her clothes with big pockets. Our hands reach into the pockets searching for treat after treat. When she goes to the big city to visit her daughters she will bring us that special sweet, that candy that she tells us everyone eats in France, the candy that will make us French. It is like the candy in our dreams bright colored and sweet, filled with coconut. She is the only one who knows where this candy can be found. It is her secret. We do not want to know. We want it to be always a surprise, always a mystery.

At her house she cooks everything on a wood-burning stove. She says that she could never get used to one of those new things. We take turns pushing the wood into the burning fire. We are fascinated by fire. I want to cook on this wood stove. I want to make daddy a cake. At home we cannot make cakes. We cannot play in the kitchen. At Big Mama's the kitchen is our home. She does not measure her ingredients. I want to know if she is sure that we are getting things right. I do not know about a pinch of this and a pinch of that. We keep opening the door to watch the cake baking. She warns us that it will fall, that it will sink like a brick in water. When it is done she warns us to take it from the oven carefully, slowly. We are too excited. We drop it. It falls in the woodpile and is covered in dust and dirt. I want to cry and cry and never stop crying. It is my first cake. It is a gift for daddy.

Big Mama says there is plenty of time in life to bake cakes, tells us about not crying over spilled milk. We love this telling. We would rather not cry. It is the punishment we fear usually when we spill things that makes us cry. Big Mama never punishes us. She always talks soothingly, quietly, laughing in between her words. We love her because she does not hide anything from us. Her pocketbook is not a secret woman world we cannot enter. We can go all through it searching for dimes and pennies. She tells us stories of our father as a young man. She is the one who gives us caring memories of him as a young boy who loved her, who waited on her hand and foot as we do, who searched her apron pockets as we do.

10

TELEVISION BELONGED TO him. He not only owned it, it existed for his pleasure. Sitting directly in front of it with his can of beer he would slowly release the hard lines like shadows covering his face, keeping the smiling happy self from showing through. They liked staring at him at these times, watching the changes. They liked seeing that he could feel pleasure, that he was not all hard, not all made of concrete. If they got in his way while he watched television his mood would suddenly change. The harsh angry side of him would emerge. Usually he would yell at their mama telling her that she was too soft with them, that she didn't teach them how to mind. Mama would begin to fuss and yell at them to show that she wasn't soft, that she was willing to punish, would punish any minute. When her punishments did not work she would threaten them with telling him, with Wait 'til daddy comes home.

Daddy came home to his chair, his beer, and his television. He liked watching sports, cheering on his favorite team. Saturdays and Sundays were the days for sports. They were not good days for children. There was no school, no one to play with, no *where* to go. They would be fine as long as the cartoons were on and he was outside washing his car, mowing the yard, working in the shed. When the time came to watch sports they would go outside but not if it was rainy or too cold. Her brother it seemed had all the fun games to play inside. He had coffee cans and mason jars filled with marbles. He would spread them on the floor making different patterns, shooting them with his favorite, his lucky one.

The father was busy watching the game, while the boy played marbles on the floor. She did not want to play with her sisters, she wanted to play with the marbles. The boy said no. She hated the way he could assert these boy rights and not include them in games. They were always being told to share. Angry at his refusal to let her play, she threatened to walk right into the marbles, scattering them everywhere. The boy dared her. Mama had already begun to encourage her to leave the boy alone. Several times the father had interrupted his game to tell her to leave him alone, that he did not want to tell her one more time to leave him alone. Again the boy dared her. She hesitated only a few seconds before stomping her feet onto his marbles. Jumping from his chair the father began to hit her—not wanting to damage his hands since he needed them for work, he tore a piece of wood from the screen door that kept flies out. As he hit her with the wood he kept saying Didn't I tell you to leave those marbles alone? Didn't I tell you? The mama stood watching, afraid of this anger, afraid of what it might do, but too afraid to stop it. The spectators knew not to cheer this punishment or they might be next. They would cheer afterward, they would tease her afterward when he could not hear, when they did not need to fear being next.

She was sent to bed without dinner. She was told to stop crying, to make no sound or she would be whipped more. No one could talk to her and she could talk to no one. She could hear him telling the mama that the girl had too much spirit, that she had to learn to mind, that that spirit had to be broken.

11

SHE HAS LEARNED to fear white folks without understanding what it is she fears. There is always an edge of bitterness, sometimes hatred, in the grown-ups' voice when they speak of them but never any explanation. When she learns of slavery in school or hears the laughter in geography when they see pictures of naked Africans—the word *savage* underneath the pictures—she does not connect it to herself, her family. She and the other children want to understand Race but no one explains it. They learn without understanding that the world is more a home for white folks than it is for anyone else, that black people who most resemble white folks will live better in that world. They have a grandmother who looks white who lives on a street where all the other people are white. She tells them things like a Black nigger is a no-good nigger, that her Papa looked like a white man but was a nigger. She never explains to them why she has married a man whose skin is the color of soot and other wonderful black things, things they love—shoe polish, coal, women in black slips. She cannot wait to grow up and be a woman who can wear black slips, black dresses. Black is a woman's color—that's what her mama tells her. You have to earn the right to wear the color black. They cannot wait to get away from this grandmother's house when she calls one of them blackie in a hating voice, in a voice that seems to say I cannot stand the sight of you. They want to protect each other from all forms of humiliation but cannot. They stand cringing and weeping inside saying nothing. They do not want to be whipped with the black leather strap with holes in it hanging on the wall. They know their place. They are children. They are black. They are next to nothing.

White folks mean little to them. They pay them no mind. It is black people of all colors who are at the center of their world. They imagine that Jesus even if he is white understands children, respects them. When they learn the words to a song "Jesus loves the little children of the world, red and yellow, black and white, they are precious in his sight," they sing it over and over again to the grownups, hoping they will hear and understand that children are precious, that they need to be valued. No one black or white seems to understand this except for a few old men.

Where they live, on hill land, they have white neighbors. They are not the good white folks, the ones who look at you with sugary smiles. They are the peckerwoods, the crackers, the ones who look at black folk with contempt and hate. Children are warned to stay away from them, to pretend not to hear when they talk, to stay away from their yards, and not to enter their houses, not for anything. All such warnings make them curious, make them desire to know more. They go to the poor white folk's house every chance they get. They see that the food they eat looks better than the food they see over there. They see that these white folk have hardly any furniture. They are visiting there one evening just before dark. The white folks are eating popcorn and drinking beer. They want some of the popcorn. She is offered popcorn in exchange for a kiss. Her brother dares her. She gives the kiss, gives him the popcorn for already she is ashamed. She knows better, knows that kisses are for friends and other loved ones. She fears the history in this exchange. White men taking black girls, black women, the word they do not understand but hear the grown-ups use: white men raping black women. After eating the popcorn he assures her that he will tell as soon as they are home, that she will be punished. Rushing home, running through the dark, she hopes the punishment will wipe away the feeling of shame.

12

MUSIC LESSONS, LIKE everything else, had to be worked for if one was poor. When she told her mama she would like to learn to play the piano they were not surprised. They had noticed the long fingers, the grace with which they moved. They were already thinking about the way in which a woman could earn a little bit of money teaching music lessons, playing for the church—money, recognition. Still they could not afford them. Her mother bargained with a music teacher down the street, lessons in exchange for baby-sitting, house cleaning, going to the store. From the very beginning she would sit at the keys silently unmoved, knowing that she would never learn to play, that she would never be a pianist. She could not tell them her feeling. They would laugh at it, brush it away like a piece of lint, step on it like they stepped on little bugs. So she kept it to herself, kept trying, kept practicing. Hearing the music that had no feeling, moving the keys up and down without understanding them—it was the experience that showed her it was not simply enough to desire. She longed to play, dreamed of making beautiful music. Her first music teacher, old and bored by the sound of children banging their fingers against the keys took sick—the lessons had to stop. Secretly she was relieved but told no one. Not even when the mama began to look around for another teacher. Not even when Miss Ruth Tandy, the light-skinned retired school teacher who lived across the street from them, expressed an interest in taking on the new pupil.

Miss Ruth Tandy interested her. She lived in a house of many rooms with a sick mother. The husband, the man who made it possible for her to be called Mrs. whenever anyone remembered, was rarely seen. Once a month they would see his car parked in front. Only now and then would they see the tall brown-skinned stranger leave, holding his hat, kissing Mrs. Ruth Tandy at the door.

Lessons at her house were an ordeal. Sitting in the living room, where dark heavy curtains prevented even the slightest bit of light from brightening their spirits, they would wait their turn, whispering now and then, writing notes. Occasionally Miss Tandy would threaten punishment if someone laughed or talked loud. As the child whose lessons were in exchange for work, it was she who left the room to see what the music teacher's mother wanted, to fetch the glass of water, the other blanket, the cool washrag. She did not mind the work. Walking through the interior of the dark rooms was like visiting a museum, everything different and strange. It was more exciting than lessons. When her turn came she would sit in that silent moment of knowing, certain that she would never be Mozart or Beethoven until she heard the sharp tongue of the music teacher, cutting across her back like a whip on the flesh of slaves picking cotton. Hitting a wrong note she thought about their aching backs, their dry throats, the hot sun. She would return again to "Swans on the Lake" as a pencil clicked against her knuckles again and again, until she got it right, until the tears stopped and she played without wonder or feeling the dream song of swans like princesses on water.

She came first at the recital, stiff in her new dress, fearful of hitting the wrong notes, of not fulfilling the promises of well-earned lessons. But when her fingers touched the keys she forgot herself, her failures, and gave her hands the freedom to see swans gliding, the freedom to make beautiful music full of the recognition that she would never play again.

13

MAMA TELLS US that it is fine to love our friends but they are not family. Family is more important than friends. We are used to family. We have grown up in family. We are not used to having friends that live nearby. Since we moved from the country to the city everything has changed. We can walk home from school with all the other kids. There are no buses. No one comes from miles and miles away. There is a girl in the third-grade class that they say looks like me, only she has lighter skin and has long hair. Maybe it is because we look alike that we decide to be friends and stay friends forever. Like me she loves to read books, is smart in class, and sometimes wears glasses. I wear glasses all the time. Saru is angry when they complain to her that they must find the money to buy me a pair of glasses. She says that the glasses will do nothing but ruin my eyesight, that she has a cure for not being able to see things far away. This time they do not listen to her. I have brought a note home from school that says I cannot read the writing on the blackboard. In the doctor's office we look at rows and rows of glasses. I want the ones that are square and black, shaped almost like dominoes. She buys the ones that are pink and shaped like the ends of wings. My new friend has a neat pair of black glasses but she does not have to wear them all the time.

Rena lives around the corner from me. The first time I ask mama if I can go to their house she wants to know who her parents are, what they do. I do not know the answer to these questions, and I do not like them. I am not planning to play with her parents. I do not dare ask why it is impor-tant to know about parents as she could become angry and say no. She says yes. I am so excited and afraid at the same time. Rena lives at the very end of Younglove Street. She walks to meet me at the corner of Younglove and Vine. She lives in a house that is painted pink. I do not tell her how much I hate the color pink. She lives with her grand-mother and sometimes her mother. When I am introduced to her grandmother she wants to know all about my people. That is easy. When I tell her who they are starting way back with Saru's mother, she tells me that Rena and I are proba-bly cousins. This excites us as we want desperately to be-long to one another. If we are cousins then we really belong.

We play croquet in the backyard, drink lemonade, and talk about books and boys. We talk about all the wonderful things we are going to do when we grow up. She is going to be a doctor and make sick people well, or a teacher, or a housewife with two children. She is an only child. She says that it is sometimes lonely. I do not tell her how lonely it can be to be one of many, especially if you do not fit in. Instead I tell her that I will be a librarian, a writer, and will never marry. She laughs at me when I say that I will never marry, and tells me of course I will. We have birthdays in the same month. We plan our parties together. Later mama says no. Birthdays at our house are for family. I am only a little disappointed. When I ask her if Rena and I are really cousins she says she cannot say, cannot remember that far back maybe Saru will know. Saru knows everything about the past.

It does not matter if we are cousins or not. We belong together. Even when boys tell us they like Rena better than me, or me better than Rena. We stick out our tongues and keep walking. We spend all our time laughing, talking about books and the future. We spend years meeting each other at the corner of Younglove and Vine.

14

NOTHING AND NO one had prepared her for death. Death, that snake that had confronted them on the way to school, walking up the same dirt road they had walked year in and year out. Death, that spider that had bitten their sleeping mother in the eye. Death, that dream she had had about the beautiful princess, the one that would not open her eyes, regain her color, move again until he kissed her. Well, in her dream death was not whatever spirit was holding the beautiful princess and keeping her still—death was what was in the air, like a smell, pervading everything, when all the little people hovering around the still body realized that he, that prince, that kissing prince, was never going to come, *that* death made her scream out in protest.

Death first came with the sickness of Sister Ray, still her father's mother. Sister Ray lived by herself so when she got poorly, as they would say, they had no choice but to offer her comfort in their home, so that mama the woman she had always thought should not have married her son, so that mama whom she had made miserable with her lies, her storytelling, could nurse her, could be by her side feeding her, washing her, comforting her, changing her bed. And it˙was that same mama who made her children get into bed one afternoon. Something had to be seriously wrong because they never had to sleep in the afternoon. They could tell that something was happening, something hard, painful, difficult to face, something terrible, something worse than monsters, dragons, or cowboys. So they fell off to sleep as soon as their little bodies were tucked into the four beds—eagerly approaching the dreams that would comfort them, take them further from the real real world where something that could not be faced was happening.

She pretended to be asleep, closing her eyes not too tightly—that's when the parent people know you are playing—but closing them softly. When the mama thought that they were all sleeping, she began to tidy everywhere in the sickroom where Sister Ray lay in the big bed. She took one of the little washbasins and began washing Sister Ray who lay still. It was like a television drama to that not-yet-sleeping six-year-old who watched fascinated, who watched all this stuff that seemed to be happening in slow motion. The part in the drama that most fascinated her, because she could not make sense out of it, could not discover what it meant, was the part where the mama took her hand and moved it gently down Sister Ray's face from forehead to chin, closing the bright eyes that had been staring out at her ever since the washing began.

It seemed like it was only a few seconds later, just when she was gathering her courage to make a sound so that the mama would come and see what was happening with her, so that she could then ask a question, that the men came, they were three or four. She knew they were men by their smell, that strange mixture of sweet cologne and alcohol. She could hear their voices even before she saw them. They walked through the room where the children were sleeping carrying something. She lifted her body to see what it was. One of them who smelled like cigarette smoke wanted to know what she was doing awake. She ignored him. She ignored the mama telling her to go back to sleep. She saw them strap the body of Sister Ray to the funny-moving bed. She saw them carry it away. She had found it all satisfying, simply fulfilling, this thing called death. Afterward she slept deeply—convinced that death need never be feared.

15

EVERY SUNDAY MISS Erma sits on the third pew. No one ever sits in her place. Even if she is late it is there waiting—a space large enough for two people. She is short and plump like our Big Mama. She walks with a cane, wears funny hats. I do not want to grow up to be a woman who wears funny hats. I think we look silly in them, silly like clowns, silly like paper party hats, silly like Halloween. I do not want to come to church looking silly, knowing that children like myself are staring, wanting to laugh, holding their mouths with their hands, rolling their eyes at one another—anything to keep the laughing sounds from coming out. We noticed her not because of her funny hats, not even because of the way that she has a special place reserved for her but because she is old, because she has long been a member of this church. She is one of the church founders.

She was there at the very beginning. From our seats in the children's choir we can tell that if she has been here from the beginning of the church 'til now—she is very old, older than we can imagine.

We notice her because during the sermon, just as the preacher is reaching the point at which what he says reaches into our hearts so that we feel it pressed against the passionate beating—she screams out in a loud and piercing voice, one long sentence. We understand the first part of it, the part where she says Thankgodthankyoujesus. We do not understand the second part. We hear her saying Thank god for hot paprika. This is forever puzzling, mysterious to us, until we grow older, until she is long dead and we come to know that what she has left piercing and ringing in our ears is a Thank god, thank you jesus for heartfelt religion. Although we know that in the home of the church god can be thanked for anything we are glad the mystery is solved—in our hearts we are glad.

Who can remember when this short plump woman wearing face powder that made it appear her skin was covered in ash first spoke to me. She is one who will tell you that she has been watching you from birth, that she has seen you grow. You stand rigid in her embrace, afraid of what it is she has seen, your young body pressed forever into her flesh as if she has died and you have been forgotten. She first spoke to me when I began reading the scripture for the morning offering, listening to my voice rising softly above the click of coins, the organ music, like smoke, drifting and settling. She waited for me after church, to hold

me in those arms, to tell me that my reading (.
preacher's sermon) also found its way into the hea
pressed itself against the beating. Because of th
wanted to give me something, some gesture of her
dence that the god voice that came out of me and tou
her beating heart would go on speaking and name itse
this world. She tells me to tell my mama to send me to
house. I become a regular visitor. Never allowed to s
long—only as long as it takes to speak a little, to be hand
the gift, the gesture of her regard, I return home soon.

Her house is clean and airy. It reminds me of bright new
pennies. When I enter, the coolness touches me like feathers, like those bright bird feathers in the funny hats. I follow
her through this house to the kitchen—where the gift awaits.
It comes in a box, a little basket, a sack. I never open it until I am all the way home. It is a wonderful and mysterious
love I must wait for the others to share.

16

TO HAVE BEEN there—at that moment when they first discovered the art of picture taking, when they first felt the magic in black boxes. When they first agreed, no not in words but in the still, erect way they held their bodies, that it was acceptable for the photographer to capture their likeness, their dress, their most intimate look. She is the woman in the black-and-white photo wearing a blue-and-green cotton dress with buttons like tiny pearls, wearing no shoes with her hair hanging, jet black, long and straight. This is what the camera does. Her hair has not been combed. It has not been plaited into the two braids that identify this woman as the grandmother I have always known. It is she who explains that picture taking is no innocent act—that it is a dangerously subtle way we drive our souls into extinction. If this is not so why is it that the

photographers always manage to arrive just when the tribe is dying out, just when the traditional practices lose power, just when the people are blinded by sorrow. She says no to picture taking—when everything is lost the pictures hardly matter, like the talking box they capture only the remnants, only what is left of life. She is only her real self when her hair is combed, sitting not standing. She is never in front of the camera.

I believe her. I see the black-and-white photo of a fat baby wearing a pink dress sitting on a bed. I know this is not me and has never been for this baby has no hair. Her skull is smooth and shiny like polished silver with black jade for eyes—this cannot be me. The grown-ups identify it as me, happy baby, smiling baby, baby with no hair. I know who I am, the one not seen in the photo, the one hiding under the bed, hiding in the dark, waiting for the camera monster to go away.

I believe her. They are making us children stand endlessly still while they take shot after shot—birthdays, Easter Sunday, Christmas. We worry about this picture taking. Can it be they will not remember what we look like. Can it be they will forget so soon. Can it be they do not worry about the saving of our souls.

They have bought a camera that is almost on the way to color, the photos will have blue and red, the patterns on our clothes will be bright. I want never to grow up, to be a cowgirl forever riding in my skirt, with matching vest and hats, with my pointed boots and my one gun. I can defend myself against any enemy. I can shoot straight. I do not kill Indians—they are family. I protect us from the enemy white man. I shoot straight. When they tell me that I must grow up, throw away my cowgirl clothes, give up my gun, surrender my boots, I appeal to the little black box. I want its magic to capture me forever this way, to never let go of my world of prairies, Indians, and frontiers. They come in the night. They take it all away. They burn it in the trash. I carry the memory of a cowgirl in my pocket—she is more beautiful than I will ever be again. I miss the gun, the shirt and vest, the hat, but the tears fall over the boots, over surrender and defeat. The black box gives me one backward glance.

Standing still, poised in anguish, I think of the beautiful girl riding a horse on the frontier, shooting straight. I am learning to be still, to give my life over to the black box. I am learning surrender.

17

SITTING AT SARU'S side as she smokes I hear about the reservations, about Indian women, the way in which the lighter-skinned black men wanted to marry them. She tells me that one of them, maybe her father, went there to find a bride, not a white-skinned bride, but a woman with skin the color of warm honey, with straight jet black hair, blacker than white folk's hair. Saru tells me that white folks and even some niggers like to make fun when a colored person says that they are part Indian but she says in those days there were many such unions, many such marriages. She talks sadly about this need in people to make other people deny parts of themselves. She tells me that a person cannot feel right in their heart if they have denied parts of their ancestral past, that this not feeling right in the heart is the cause of much pain. When she was a little girl black people remembered their homes in Africa, spoke languages different from English, and understood many things about life that white folks did not understand. She said they stopped talking about Africa because that was how the white folks wanted it. Saru thinks that black people could talk about their Indian kin because they knew them in the present, that this was a heritage other than slavery to lay claim to. She lays claim to it. She tells me the stories over and over so I will know them, so I will pass them on.

One story troubles my sleep. I do not tell her. I do not want her to know. I am afraid she will think I am not ready, not old enough to bear the stories. This story is about a magic woman who lives inside smoke. She hides in the smoke so no one can capture her. Smoke is to her what clay is to the red bird god. She can take the smoke and make it become many things. Using the smoke she turns herself into a male. She must be male to be a warrior. There are no women warriors. She fights fiercely against her enemies. They cannot understand when the arrows that pierce her body do not cause her to fall. When they try to capture her alive she takes the smoke wherever she can find it, in a dying fire, in the residue of a gunshot, from pipes, and turns the smoke into a snake that devours her enemies. Sometimes she turns the smoke into a bird of prey, a hawk or an owl, and sometimes a black wolf.

In my sleep I have seen the magic woman fighting battles, shooting her arrow into enemy after enemy. The part of the dream that troubles my sleep, the part I do not like to tell Saru is that the face of the young male warrior looks like my face. I stare into his eyes as if I am looking into a mirror. When Saru changes herself into a woman she no longer looks like me. To keep silent about this dream is to not understand its meaning. Saru has told me many times that dreams are messages sent to us by guardian spirits, that the wise one learns to listen to the message, to follow its wisdom.

When I tell Saru of my dream, of the young warrior who wears my face in battle, she says that this is the face of my destiny, that I am to be a warrior. I do not understand. I do not intend to fight in wars or battles. She says that there are many battlegrounds in life, that I will live the truth of the dream in time.

18

SARU CALLS THEM the People of the First Snow. I call them Indians. I tell her we learn at school that they are Indians, that like the Africans, they are called savages in our books. She tells me that we go to school to learn the white man's ways, to learn to deny parts of ourselves. She is proud of the fact that she was taken out of school to begin work while still a young girl. Her world is outside. She needs to have her fingers in the soil, to touch dirt. She tells me this is part of her mother's legacy. From her mother she learned to trap small animals, rabbits, possums, coons. She does not like coon meat. It is tough and greasy even when soaked in brine. We both love to eat fried rabbit. From her mother she learned ways to make things grow. Her tomatoes hang on the vines red and juicy. She says it has to do with all the good things she does to the dirt. We are in her garden picking beans. My back is tired and aching but she will not let me stop. From her mother she learns to keep worms for fishing. She shows me the dark damp places in the earth where we can dig deep and expect to find fishing worms. We hold them and watch them move in our hands. We keep them in dirt-filled coffee cans. People come by to buy a can of worms when they want to fish.

Saru rises early to go fishing. She has a long bamboo pole and all the worms she needs. When she is old and cannot travel long distances she walks to the creek. They find her lying there among the worms and the day's catch. They carry her home. They tell her that she must learn to accept that she is old. She knows that she is old. She is thinking of a time when the old were allowed to go their way, to die in peace, alone in the world. She tells me that she sees death all the time, standing beside her, watching her from behind this curtain. She tells me that she is not afraid, that she is ready to die.

Now that she is old she talks often to me about god. She tells me that believing in god has nothing to do with going to church. I love to hear her talk about the way she went to church and found that people were more concerned with talking about what you were wearing and who you were with and decided never to go again. She is a woman of spirit, a woman of strong language, a fighter. She tells me that she has inherited this fighting spirit from her mother, that I may have a little of it but it is too early to tell.

When she is not fighting she is quietly making quilts. Sewing the small pieces of fabric together eases her mind. Her eyesight is not what it used to be so she is not always sewing—only in the morning. She has a room filled with threads and cloth, with an old black Singer sewing machine that she works by hand and foot. Her house has many rooms that have been added, as if no thought was given to where they would go. In the sewing room she pulls back the mattress of a feather mattress made firm by layers and layers of quilts that rest under it. I select the quilt of my choice, the Star of David pattern. She tells me that it was one of the first quilts she made as a young bride. I imagine each part of the star, each different bit of cotton, has been stitched with the intensity of her love and will to make this marriage work, make it complete and fulfilling like the quilt. With my hands I trace the pattern. She tells me a woman learns patience making quilts.

19

THIS AUNT FROM my daddy's side comes for us in her big car. I am not sure I want to go to her house but I go anyway. By dusting her furniture I can make a little money. She is never pleased with my work: that is why I hate to go. Her husband is no longer alive. I always take particular care when I dust his photograph. He looks glamorous and slick. His lips shine as if he is wearing lipstick. Unlike some women, Aunt Charley is no longer interested in men. She is mainly concerned with god, piano music, and her beauty parlor business. She has turned her kitchen into a beauty parlor. Smells of bacon cooking mingle with the odor of grease and burning hair. Her beauty parlor is not a space where women come together to gossip and enjoy themselves. She does not approve of gossip. They can talk about many things in her house but they cannot talk about other folk's business. They are silent. Every now and then someone talks about the good sermon so-and-so preached on Sunday.

Aunt Charley likes talking about god and the Bible. She has a Bible sitting right near the stove amid the jars of Dixie Peach and Vaseline, near the trays filled with combs of all sizes and colors. One of my jobs is to clean this tray of combs. I must stand on a stool to reach the unusually high sink. Aunt Charley is a tall big-boned woman. Everything in her house is arranged to remind you that it is hers. It is at her house that I discover the lovely smell of Ivory Soap. The soap in our house comes in thick brown pieces that look more like stones than something one would use to wash the body. Lye soap comes from Saru's house. We do not understand that we use it not because it is the best soap but because it is free. We do not understand money. We do not understand how quickly a bar of Ivory Soap disappears. We know that lye soap lasts forever. We talk about how we will not use any lye soap when we grow up. We will have the best, only the sweet smelling. I will have only this milky white Ivory Soap. Things that smell too sweet tend to make it hard for me to breathe, give me the feeling that I am on the verge of having an asthma attack. The subtle fragrance in the Ivory Soap makes it special to me. We would never think to take the bits and pieces of it home. We do not steal. We know better. She never gives us any even though she hears us admiring it. Her customers pay her cash on the spot. Before they leave they can wash their hands with the soap. They can use the clean towels that hang near the sink. We wash our hands in another part of the house.

After all the customers leave we sweep the floor. We know that there are many magical things that can be done with hair. Customers know it, too. Sometimes they will bring little brown paper sacks to put their hair in after it is cut. Some say it will make the hair grow to burn it. I want them to burn it on the spot for I am fascinated by the way hair burns. They never burn it on the spot. Other people are careful to take their hair so no enemy will get it and use it to work an evil charm. Aunt Charley says that is all nonsense. We know not to believe her. We know magic is real. We take all the hair and put it in the trash. It will all be burned. Even though she is always fixing hair, Aunt Charley likes wigs. We like to go into her bedroom when she is busy and try on all the wigs, the red ones, the black ones. We cannot understand why women wear wigs, especially women with lots of hair. Wigs remind us of doll hair, of unliving things. We do not want to look dead.

20

SARU DOES NOT read or write. It is not that she does not think these things are important. It is that she has never had the time. She has always been busy. She lives in the old ways. She does not buy everything from the store. When you go to her house anything may be happening. They may be making lye soap, butter, or wine. They may be wringing the necks of chickens. The sight of her eldest daughter whirling a chicken in the air without blinking, without feeling moved by its cries and scattered feathers convinces me that in every way women are the equals of men. She washes the blood from her hands without paying any attention to it, unmoved by the scent of death. The men understand this, too. They do not wring the necks of chickens. They hunt with dogs and guns. Their prey will be placed neatly in a sack. It is the women who will look at it, who will prepare it. Her chickens are raised in the backyard. They have names and some are special to her. I want to know how it is she can bear to destroy something that she has given a name, that she has come to have feeling for. She tells me that the feeling is real but does not get in the way of destiny. She raises chickens to eat. It is a way that everyone survives. She knows to show gratitude to the chicken for giving its life. When I slip my hands under the hens to see if there are eggs I am thrilled. I gather the eggs carefully in my basket. I am excited by this knowledge of where eggs really come from, by the smells in the chicken coop, by the sounds.

At Saru's house there is a special room for the storage of food—the pantry. It was the most important place before the invention of refrigerators. She refuses to accept this change, continuing to store everything there. There are special days for canning, for putting up green beans, peaches, for making pickles, preserves. We rarely come to visit during these working days for mama refuses to bring us. She cannot stand the heat in the kitchen, the flies, the smells. She cannot stand the old ways.

To us children the pantry is most important because it is a good hiding place. A little body squeezed in the dark beside sacks of Osh potatoes, between gunnysacks filled with nuts and dried fruit is hard to find. Sometimes even to the little person hiding there the still shapes of hanging smoked meat, whole hams, make shadows that are large and frightening. There may be treats in the pantry. She scolds us for playing there.

At Saru's house food is serious business. There they

make the kind of food I like best nearly every day: greens, corn bread, and fried corn. Her corn bread is made in the old way, not with milk and eggs but with a little animal fat, hot water, and salt mixed together then deep-fried. This is the way the old ones made their bread she tells me. This is the only bread to eat. The tasteless white stuff that comes in the plastic packages makes her sick. She says she understands why people are so poorly if they try and survive eating such stuff. When she is in a giving mood Saru makes pans of mush to be fried. It is the most delicious taste in the world, better than any sweet. It is her treat. She does not make cookies, she makes something that looks like a mixture of biscuit and cookie, which she calls a tea cake. Her kitchen is filled with strings of hot red peppers she has grown and dried. She tells me that the best way to live in the world is to learn to make things grow. I am ashamed when all my little plants die.

21

WE KNOW THAT children are not born innocent or good. We know that children are able to hurt each other and even grown-ups. We know that some children like to hurt. I do not want to hurt. I do not even want to fight. They act as if this is another sign that I am not normal. It is seen as normal for children to play with hurting. I do not want to play. When I am finally forced to fight I do not play. It is a real life and death matter for me. I am aware of the seriousness of it all, the threat. I respond. Across the fence are neighbors with children. A fight has been arranged between me and the girl that is my age or a little older. Since I fight "wild" it will be fun to watch. I try to avoid the fight but cannot. We forget our friendship for the play. The blows we strike at one another hurt. The blood that flows from our nose is red and wet. It is not the play blood on the toy soldiers, on the patients that the doll nurse waits on. The fight is stopped by grown-ups at their house who scream at us to go home and stay there. I am glad it is over. I am glad that we can no longer play with one another. Months pass and we must stay on our side of the fence and they must stay on their side. Slowly the friendships begin again.

Fighting between children annoys the grown-ups only if someone is seriously hurt or if they must go to the doctor and money must be paid. Fights annoy the grown-ups when clothes are torn. Clothes cost money. There is more fighting when the schools attended by all black children are closed down and we must walk long distances to the schools in white neighborhoods. In the park on the way home from the junior high a fight begins every day. Sometimes between white and black but mainly between black and black. A younger sister is always fighting. The grown-ups urge her to stop. They do not understand how difficult it is to stop when the other children are pushing, threatening, abusing. They do not care. They are concerned for the clothes, the body wounds that may cost money. They do not want to understand why the fighting takes place. I was never there. I only heard about it. I never knew the cause. I never understood.

At home with one another we are not allowed to fight. Mama tells us she will not raise a household full of children who grow up hating one another, fighting one another. She will not have it even if she has to kill us all to make peace. When I threaten one of her other children with a knife she no longer protests the fighting but stops it to threaten me with the consequences of hurting any of her children. She thinks I am crazy, that I do not fight fair. I do not understand the meaning of fair when one is fighting because someone else forces you to, when fighting is not your choice. We are punished for the fighting. I am punished more for acting as if the fighting is real.

At school someone is hit in the head with a brick. Their body lies still and motionless until the grown-ups come. The head bleeds. They warn us all about the danger of fighting. They still act as though it is a normal, an inevitable part of life. They do not know what to say when a child takes a gun lying around his house and shoots another child. They hear that the two boys were fighting. They hear that one ran and got the gun, pointed it at the other and killed him dead. They hear he thought the gun was empty.

22

TO HER CHILD mind old men were the only men of feeling. They did not come at once smelling of alcohol and sweet cologne. They approached one like butterflies, moving light and beautiful, staying still for only a moment. She found it easy to be friends with them. They talked to her as if they understood one another, as if they were the same—nothing standing between them, not age, not sex. They were the brown-skinned men with serious faces who were the deacons of the church, the right-hand men of god. They were the men who wept when they felt his love, who wept when the preacher spoke of the good and faithful servant. They pulled wrinkled handkerchiefs out of their pockets and poured tears in them, as if they were pouring milk into a cup. She wanted to drink those tears that like milk would nourish her and help her grow.

One of those men walked with his body bent, crippled. The grown-ups frowned at her when she asked them why he didn't walk straight. Did he know how to walk straight? Had he ever learned? They never answered. Every Sunday he read the scripture for the main offering. His voice wrinkled like paper. Sometimes it sounded as if there were already tears in it waiting to spill over, waiting to wet the thirsty throats of parched souls. She could not understand the reading. Only one part was clear. It was as though his voice suddenly found a message that eased sorrow, a message brighter than any tear. It was the part that read, It is required and understood that a man be found faithful. He was one of the faithful.

She loved the sight of him. After church she would go and stand near him, knowing that he would give her his hand, covered old bones in wrinkled brown skin that reminded her of a well-worn leather glove. She would hold that hand tight, never wanting to give it back. In a wee pretend voice full of tears and longing he would ask for his hand back saying all the while that he would love for her to keep it but could not build his house without it. She loved to hear him talk about the house that he had been building for years, a dream house, way out in the country, with trees, wildflowers, and animals. She wanted to know if there were snakes. He assured her that if she came to visit the snakes would come out of their hiding places just for her, singing and playing their enchanted flutes.

It was a hot, hot day when she went to his house. She

came all by herself slowly walking down the dirt road, slowing moving up the hill. He stood at the top waiting. The house was so funny she couldn't stop laughing, it was half finished. She could not imagine how anyone could live in a half-finished house. He gave her his hand, strong and brown. She could see it sawing, nailing, putting together boards that contained the memories of all his unfulfilled dreams. She could see the loneliness in that hand. When she whispered to him that she always held that hand—the right one—because all the loneliness was stored there like dry fruit in a cool place, he understood immediately.

Sitting on the steps watching him work she could ask all the questions about being crippled that she had ever wanted to know. Was he alone because he was crippled. Was he not married because he was crippled. Was he without children because he was crippled. Her questions smoothed the wrinkles in his brow, took the tears from his voice, wet his dreams with the promise of a woman waiting faithfully with outstretched hands.

23

NO WINE TASTES as good as that which Saru makes. We pick the purple grapes for her from the vines in our backyard. This is before daddy tears the grape arbor down to keep strangers from coming into the yard eating them. When we first see the grape arbor we cannot believe it. We had never seen grapes growing. It is also a good hiding place, a good place to play house. We cannot believe that he will chop it down. He does. Saru finds other grapes for her wine. We do not like the wine that the grown-ups buy in bottles. It tastes bitter, not sweet and thick with fruit like Saru's wine. They let us drink a little. They tell us that we must learn to drink in moderation, properly so that we will not grow up to drink to excess. The grown-ups like to party and drink. We know this because we once lived in a flat above a nightclub. At night when we should be sleeping we can hear the sounds of drinking people. We can smell the odors on our father's breath, on the breath of his men friends who want to kiss us, who want to tell us how cute we are. We are too young to know what drinking means. We are not too young to understand when they tell mama that this is not a good place to be raising children. We are not surprised when we move. No more music. No more bright lights. No more drinking sounds.

Friday is the day to drink. It is the day when working people begin to try and give themselves back the pleasure that the job has taken away. We do not like the beginning of these days when people begin to change, become something else so as to reassure themselves that the white folk have not taken away all their powers to create. We do not like the way they change because the tenderness, the smiles, the laughter are all fleeting, will fade. We watch the grown-ups begin in laughter and end in tears. We stare at their tears. We see that they are in pain. We do not trust the other grown-ups when they dismiss it all by saying they are just drunk. We imagine that drinking is like walking a tightrope.

We never hear the word alcoholic. Even though we know there are women and men who bring their sipping bags with them wherever they go. We know they are hiding bottles in the neat brown paper sacks that remind us of freshly ironed shirts with starch in the collar. We know that some of them begin drinking early in the morning, that they cannot help themselves. Saru says that she has never liked drink, that she has seen it bring many a strong man down. It is she that tells us that not all folk take to liquor in the same way. It is she that notices that the ghosts are able to drink more than black or Indian folk without the drink making them wild or crazy. We go crazy with drink she says, pointing to her daughter who is quiet and patient in her work during the week. After her first sip on the weekends she is angry, cursing, bitter. Everyone stays out of her way. They accept the drinking. They see it as her only pleasure. They do not try and invent other pleasures.

We watch them sink into drink as if it is a feather mattress, as if it is a clear clean lake, like Blue Lake, one that will carry them, keep them afloat. We learn early to say no when they ask us to go to the store with the note that will bring someone closer to loss, closer to no longer remembering who they are.

24

WHEN SHE GAVE herself to god she was not afraid. She was so sure he wanted her, had lain awake nights wondering when this soul like a ripened plum would wet his holy bed with unforgiveable sweetness. She was sure that there was joy to be found in being wanted long before her mama decided that it was time she and her brother joined the church. She knew she was ready to be the bride of god, ready to shed her blood in his honor and for his name. Mama gave them their instructions. They were not to join during the morning services. When the preacher asked in that tender voice for all those souls longing for god, needing him, to come, to give them themselves—they were not to answer. They were to wait for revival, for the special week when a new preacher comes to do the service, when children and grown-ups walk down the aisle night after night saying yes, yes, yes—they wanted to be saved. In her bed at night she moved restlessly to the sound of their chanting yes, yes, yes—she wanted to be saved.

When their turn came, she sat next to her brother, slowly becoming the little sister he and the grown-ups had always wanted her to be. She had never liked crowds. She had never faced a crowd waiting to hear her confess secrets, to tell of her personal rendezvous with god. Her legs shook as she followed her brother down the aisle, her heart beat fast, loud, so loud that not even the preacher's smile—as he placed his hand in her hand, asking her did she love the lord, did she want him for her personal savior, did she want salvation—could give her speech. All the lines she had rehearsed, the pretty words that would describe her nightly meeting with god, their walks in the garden, the waiting for him near bushes of pink and white baby roses, the moist dew that sometimes caught in her hair, the way he warmed her hands with breath that smelled of honeysuckle and jasmine—all the words would not come. In place of words she gave them tears, the same tears that had wet his wounds, that like warm summer rain had caressed his flesh with everlasting love. Later, when her mama asked why she stood there crying like a baby, saying nothing, not opening her big mouth, she still refused to speak. She did not say they were holy tears, water that will heal and renew. She was waiting to tell him all.

They were to wear white, all white, gown, slip, panties, cap. She wanted god to see her as he had always seen her, naked, brown, her flesh moving in the darkness like dusk, like the moment before the call to morning prayer. She was afraid he would not know her in white. She felt ashamed to meet him this one time in so public a place. She was sure it meant an end to all the private love they shared, the secret meetings. She entered the dark church slowly. Seeing no one yet, hearing their voices sing of water that will be troubled, of wading in the water. She searched the night for some sign of his face. The cold water held her trembling flesh, took away her ability to wander aimlessly, searching. She was no longer free to seek, to come and go whenever she chose, he had dropped a net in the water, to capture her, to hold her, to make her holiness his own.

The brown hands of John the Baptist were about her— John, beheaded friend and lover. He spoke with the voice of a stranger. His words an alien tongue. Taking this his sister, he baptized her in the name of the father, the son, and the holy ghost. Only her anguished cry pierced the dark with knowledge of this betrayal.

25

COUNTRY CHURCHES WERE the places where folk just went wild with religion—singing, shouting, praying, praising the lord all over the place. Those churches never had air conditioners, no it was as if the lord kept them from getting enough money just to sweat the sin out of them, just to make the overweight ladies faint, just so the ushers could give out those paper fans, the only beautiful printed images of black people we ever saw—because those fans had been donated by black businesses, the funeral home, the cabstand. When black people paid we knew that we really wanted to see reflections of the world we lived in, not someone else's world. Even more wilder than the country churches were the tent meetings, held by the visiting evangelists from the Holy Roller churches. We thought maybe they were evangelists rather than preachers 'cause women could speak the word of god at their services, could preach. In our Baptist church we had learned women were not supposed to preach, were not worthy enough to even cross the threshold of god's annointed space—the pulpit.

I must always remind myself just as my feet begin to move across that place to go back, to walk behind the chairs, because I am female, because I can never be truly holy. I want to go to the churches where women can preach, where god is calling women to come and talk. Mama wants me and all of us to stay away—she does not want us to be tempted, to be seduced. I go anyway—when the tent meeting is around the corner. She says Just this one time. I want to tell her that I am afraid but I cannot, afraid that just by my going there god might call me, might ask me to speak. There they speak in tongues, in holy languages no one can understand. I want to be a believer. I want to hear it for myself. The night I go it is especially crowded, especially hot. The preacher is a man. I am disappointed. He tells the story of the money lenders in the temple. Sitting astride a chair pretending it is a horse, he moves around the church waving a colored handkerchief showing us how Jesus made the unholy flee the temple, flee his sacred place. I watch fascinated, unbelieving. God has failed to call me. Everyone else is moved. Their feet pat the ground, the pews rock. I feel the walls close in on me, only there are no walls. I feel I, too, want to flee the temple. When I move they think the spirit has touched me, is holding me close, leading me toward the altar where all must be laid; I am heading for the opening in the tent, rushing home in the night air, convinced that the country churches are better than an old tent meeting.

At the country churches you get baptized outside in the creek. My father was baptized outside. They had prayed for his restless unbelieving soul for a long time. The soul of a grown man is hard to move, to touch. They prayed for the grown man, husband, father, who had not yet found it possible to put his hand in god's hand, who was not saved. I wonder how salvation finally came to him. If the walls of history, tradition, family, had suddenly closed in, had terrified him so that he cried out and then they knew. They knew by the sound of his cries that he would open himself to salvation, would enter the water a stranger and return a child of god. His mama is overjoyed that he has seen the light. She weeps as he moves into the water, as his body goes under in the name of the father, the son, and the holy ghost. I watch amazed, sure the water will betray him, will hold him under. When he rises a new man, I do not join the shouts of victory.

26

WHEN I GROW up I cannot say what I want to be. I cannot say that I do not want to grow up. I am a child who is sad all the time. They tell us children should be happy, should love to go outside and play. I would rather read books. There have always been books in our house even when we were very young. I remember daddy reading paperback novels, detective stories. I know he reads dirty books because I read them, too. I know that there are black writers like James Baldwin, Frank Yerby, and Ann Petry because their books are on the shelf. They tell me that these books are for when I am older. When we leave the country and move to the city we have a library to go to. We have a library period. This is my favorite time. I love biographies. I read about George Washington Carver, Mary McLeod Bethune, Booker T. Washington, Louisa

May Alcott, Amelia Earhart, Abraham Lincoln. We are not allowed to take books home. There is no money to replace them if they are lost. I am a good reader, careful with books, a library helper. I take as many books home as I like. I read Laura Ingalls Wilder's *Little House on the Prairie* and Alcott's *Little Women*—and every other Alcott book. I find remnants of myself in Jo, the serious sister, the one who is punished. I am a little less alone in the world.

Mama buys me a hardback book of religious stories. She buys it from a traveling salesman, a white man. The only white men we see in our neighborhoods are selling something, insurance, products. Daddy thinks it is a waste to spend money on books for a child. Mama thinks I should be given a good book to read, a book that is all my own. I am thrilled. I go house to house reading to invalids and shut-ins. This is good missionary work. This is part of being a christian. I do not wish to be a missionary. I love to read. I like reading to other people but I like best to read silently in a quiet room alone, just me and the book. When I become the problem child they blame it all on the books. They make me stop reading unless all my chores are done. They make me stop reading to go outside and play. They snatch the book out of my hand and throw it away because I am not listening when someone is talking to me.

Mrs. Mayes, a retired schoolteacher, calls our house to say she is spring cleaning, throwing away books that I can have if I come and get them. I do not like the long walk to her house. I cannot walk alone so I must wait until someone can go with me. When we arrive she has already thrown the books away. I must stand on a wooden box to get them out of the trash. My hands are dusty. My sister refuses to help. Inside the trash are cartons of tiny books called *A Little Leather Library*. They can be carried in the pocket. The green leather covers have become dry and brittle. The works of Shakespeare, Homer, Dickens, and all the Romantics are there. The novels of George Eliot, the Brontës, the poetry of Poe and Emily Dickinson. We have a hard time carrying the cartons. They smell of mold and decay but to me they are a treasure. The print is so tiny I am sure it will take hours to read each little line but I am ready. When we get home they say More trash but they are happy because I am happy.

The books are a new world. I am even less alone.

27

LIES ARE LIKE bombs, I tell myself. They explode into the air shattering everything in sight, bits and pieces of our lives. I want to tell the truth. I want to say this is how it really is yet when I tell the truth they never accept it. It never fits with anything they want to hear. When I tell them a lie, when we lie to them, they punish us. The punishment is harsher, crueler than for other crimes. There is an art to lying, to telling one's story in such a way that it can be believed. I tried once or twice to change my story, but it did not work, the trembling of my lips, the inadequacy of my speech, always alerts them to my failure. The other children look at me with scorn. I cannot be let in on the various deceptions because I cannot maintain the cover of truth, cannot prevent punishment.

We learn that there is a word for people who are sick

with lying, who cannot help themselves, like people who are sick with drink or sick with TB. The word has more than four, even more than six letters. We quickly forget how to say it but its meaning stays with us; it is possible to be sick with lying. What we do not understand is whether or not it is possible to inherit the sickness, to get it from one's family. We could hear the grown-ups say That so-and-so is a big liar just like her daddy. We want to know all the inner secrets of a person who lies. Whether or not they feel satisfied, truly content when someone believes their lie, the way you feel after eating a good meal. We want to know if the feeling is more one of power, of being like a god, able to make other people respond and react at one's will. These, as always, are the unanswered questions.

We are not able to punish grown-ups for their lies. We are not even allowed to tell them that they are lying. Once when I said, not thinking, not watching my every word, that so-and-so was sure a liar I was hit across the mouth. Sometimes the grown-ups could be heard talking about the preachers and how they stand right up there in the pulpit and lie. This makes the grown-ups laugh. It confuses us since we know that god loves truth. We do not under- ‹ stand why it is the good men of god who stand and lie are not struck down by a bolt of lightning or some other heaven-sent magic. It is confusing, strange and crazy making. Despite the confusion we try to be true.

Sometimes one of us, even the ones that are more skillful at telling tales, will be caught. Like crowds of people that travel for miles to watch hangings, beheadings, and other such public murders, as well as whippings, we will stand and be the audience, the excited spectators when one of us is being punished. One evening after we had all gone to bed except for one sister who was not home yet from baby-sitting, we heard the grown-ups talk about where she was, when she would be getting home. We heard the concern in the mother's voice, the anger in the father's. We knew something was wrong, that she was maybe not found where she was supposed to be. When she finally arrived home we were glad. The lights could be turned off—we could sleep. They were not satisfied. They wanted her version of where she had been and what she had been doing. Somewhere, somehow, the truth of her lie began to seep out like rainwater slowly moving through an unidentified leak. Nearly naked in her bed clothes he beat her, yelling all the while, Don't you ever lie to me. We hate the lies that make this public humiliation possible. We hate the liar. We cannot sleep until all fragments from the bomb are gathered together and thrown away. In our dreams the father is the man who places bombs in the little box, who keeps them from exploding.

28

TWO BLACK DOCTORS take care of everyone in our community. Their offices are crowded with suffering people. There is little time for anything but work, though now and then someone stops to chat, to discuss whatever it is that is ailing them. There is one black hospital. We go there only if we are critically ill, because there are only a small number of beds, a short staff. When I go to the doctor's office, not because I am sick, but with an adult who must see the doctor, I try not to breathe the smells of disinfectant, of cleaning solutions. They make me think of death and decay, that it is being hidden, covered up. I like to watch the nurses. To me they are beautiful, intelligent, capable— everything the doctors are not. I think this because the doctors are men and the nurses women. It is the nurses who combine medicine with the recognition that they are treating human beings, with human needs. It is the nurse who sympathizes with me because of the asthma attacks that keep me awake at night sitting in a dining room chair alone in the dark, unable to breathe. It is the nurse who understands that the dark hides the fear of death that is on my face, hides the fear in my chest that takes my breath away. The doctor touches me like I once touched a frog I was dissecting with sharp, pointed instruments in biology class. All the while I tried to ignore that the object I was dissecting was once living and breathing frog life, in water, making sounds. I shut down the part of me that understands that the frog has a soul that has not escaped even though the frog has died, a soul that needs care.

I cannot speak to the soul of the frog in the biology class so I deny its existence all together. Like the doctor denies mine when he is touching me, when he is asking me to breathe in and out over and over again, when he presses his cold hands on my chest. His hands are cold because he is afraid. He wants to hide from this living person. He does not want to know what really hurts me. He must see me quickly and move on to other patients. It is the only way he can make a good living, more money. Many people will not pay him. He will see them anyway. He will work long, long hours. The tiredness and desperation will show in his face. Seeing this we forgive him for shutting down that part of himself that feels for and with us. We are relieved when he takes a day off.

Whenever we can we try to avoid seeing doctors. We try

to heal ourselves at home. For my asthma, my grand-mother says, I need to chew the waxy part, the honeycomb from bees. Bits of honey in the honeycomb sweeten the pain that I am feeling. For our acne she tells us to wash our face in pee. We do not want to try this remedy even though she tells us it will work. When no remedy makes the asthma better I must go to the doctor's office. In more ways than one I am a problem child, always trouble, always sick. The doctor wants to give me a shot in my hand, I do not want it. I do not want him to touch my piano-playing hands, my long, loving fingers. I hide them in my pockets, behind my back, hold them tightly so that he can see I do not want him touching them. He smiles at me and says he will let the nurse give the shots this time. I offer her the hands, knowing she will take time to smooth the fear out of them before the needle enters.

29

HIS SMELLS FILL my nostrils with the scent of happiness. With him all the broken pieces of my heart get mended, put together again bit by bit. He can always tell when I am sad. He will ask me What have they been doing to you now. He knows that I am a wounded animal, that they pour salt on the open sores just to hear me moan. He tells me that in the end it will come out all right. He tells me Blessed are they that mourn for they shall be comforted. I am comforted by his presence. Soot-black-skinned man with lines etched deep in his face as if someone took a knife and carved them there. He is Daddy Gus, mama's father. From her I know that he has always been gentle, that he has never been a man of harsh words. I need his presence in my life to learn that all men are not terrible, are not to be feared. He, too, is one of the faithful, one of the right-hand men of god. When he speaks I listen very carefully to hear what is said. His voice comes from some secret place of knowing, a hidden cave where the healers go to hear messages from the beloved.

In my dream we run away together, hand in hand. We go to the cave. To enter we must first remove all our clothes, we must wash, we must rub our body with a red mud. We cover ourselves so completely that we are no longer recognizable as grandfather granddaughter. We enter without family ties or memory. The cave is covered with paintings that describe the way each animal has come to know that inside all of us is a place for healing, that we have only to discover it. Each animal searches and searches until they find the opening of the cave. As soon as they enter, the mind ceases, they feel at peace. They feel they are no longer blind, that they see for the first time. It is too much for the heart to bear. They stand together weeping, sobbing. When we enter the cave we also take time to weep, to lose ourselves in sorrow. We make a fire. In the fire are all the lost spirits that show us ways to live in the world. I do not yet have a language with which to speak with them. He knows. He speaks. I am the silent one, the one who bears witness. In the dream we leave the cave in quiet. Just as we reach the outside he begins talking to me without opening his mouth. He places his voice inside my head telling me that knowledge of the cave can be given to anyone, only they must be seeking, that until I can tell a seeker from someone who is just curious I must not speak about it.

We are again grandfather and granddaughter. My visits to him are frequent. He has a favorite chair by the stove in the living room. When I was much smaller I sat there cuddled in his lap like a cat, hardly moving, hardly alive so near to the stillness of death was the bliss I knew in his arms. His room is filled with treasures. Once the curtain has been drawn at the doorway so that the others cannot see, he tells me that everything has life, a tiny soul inside it—things like pocketknives, coins, bits of ribbon. He is always finding the treasures people have lost or abandoned. He hears their small souls crying in the wilderness. He gives them a place to rest. In his room treasures are everywhere. Every object has a story. He teaches me to listen to the stories things tell, to appreciate their history. He has many notebooks, little black notebooks filled with faded yellow paper. I understand from him that the notebooks are a place for the storage of memory. He writes with a secret pencil; the pages seem covered in ash, the ash left by the fire we have visited. This fire he says now burns inside us.

30

THERE IS MUCH to celebrate about being old. I want to be old as soon as possible for I see the way the old ones live—free. They are free to be different—unique—distinct from one another. None of them are alike. Some of them were already on their way to being old when I was born. I do not know them young. I do not have to forgive them past mistakes. They have not caused me any sorrow. My grandfather tells me that all he ever wanted was for the world to leave him be, that it won't let you be when you are a young man. The world demands that you work for it, make families, provide, take no time to listen to your own heart beating. He tells me that he could not accept much of what the world had to offer men, especially the business of going to war. All his sons who became soldiers lost parts of themselves. He tells me that there is no way one can kill another and not lose part of oneself. He tells me that he would not go to war, that he refused to fight. I want to know the details, why was he not drafted, why did no one force him to serve. He is indignant that I would suggest he could be forced to do anything against his will. He tells me that no one can make you do anything against your will.

The people in this house think of him as a coward, a small man shrinking into his chair like a shadow. They make fun of him, of his clothes, of his habits. They think all his treasures are junk. They have never heard their hearts beating. He has heard his—hearing this sound above all other sounds he is not provoked by their endless ridicule or attack. Sometimes in the midst of it all he reaches for his hat. He moves toward the door slowly, not even suggesting by a hurried walk that he has had enough. They do not follow him.

He is a man who does odd jobs. He works mainly for white folks, retired ladies who come out of their houses and speak to him as if he was ten years old, demanding that he cut the yard, empty their trash. He never looks them in the face. He never pays them any mind. They are he says only ghosts. He does not believe in ghosts. He works slowly, the sound of his heart setting the rhythm.

The day that his odd job is to burn trash in a nearby white lady's yard he feels tired and uncertain. The wind blows. He knows it is not a good day to burn trash but he does so anyway. He listens to his heart, beating unsteady, beating out a new rhythm. He knows that his end is near. He will not fight death. He has never been a soldier. He will give himself over to it freely. When the flames reach his body he does not notice. He does not smell the burning clothes. He has lost all memory. He has entered the cave. She notices—Miss White Lady. She notices that in her backyard an old man with a face like soot is surrounded in flames. She panics not knowing who she can call to meet the needs of an old black man on fire. She calls his home. A grandchild comes running, jumps high fences, breaks bushes, puts out the flames with his hands. These are love's hands. They can do anything. He has heard the sound of this old man's heart beating. He has been comforted by his presence. In this moment he is able to fully return that love. He will never know such honor again.

They must travel many miles to the hospital where burns are treated. Those who love him sit nearby listening to his heart. A person on fire often dies not from the flames but from a heart attack as the pain is so intense. His heart does not fail him. It knows the fire is not his enemy. It knows there is a secret in the flames that is ongoing and everlasting.

31

GOOD HAIR—THAT'S the expression. We all know it,
begin to hear it when we are small children. When we are
sitting between the legs of mothers and sisters getting our
hair combed. Good hair is hair that is not kinky, hair that
does not feel like balls of steel wool, hair that does not take
hours to comb, hair that does not need tons of grease to
untangle, hair that is long. Real good hair is straight hair,
hair like white folk's hair. Yet no one says so. No one says
Your hair is so nice, so beautiful because it is like white
folk's hair. We pretend that the standards we measure our
beauty by are our own invention—that it is questions of
time and money that lead us to make distinctions between
good hair and bad hair. I know from birth that I am lucky,
lucky to have hair at all for I was bald for two years, then
lucky finally to have thin, almost straight hair, hair that
does not need to be hot-combed.

We are six girls who live in a house together. We have different textures of hair, short, long, thick, thin. We do not appreciate these differences. We do not celebrate the variety that is ourselves. We do not run our fingers through each other's dry hair after it is washed. We sit in the kitchen and wait our turn for the hot comb, wait to sit in the chair by the stove, smelling grease, feeling the heat warm our scalp like a sticky hot summer sun.

For each of us getting our hair pressed is an important ritual. It is not a sign of our longing to be white. It is not a sign of our quest to be beautiful. We are girls. It is a sign of our desire to be women. It is a gesture that says we are approaching womanhood—a rite of passage. Before we reach the appropriate age we wear braids and plaits that are symbols of our innocence, our youth, our childhood. Then we are comforted by the parting hands that comb and braid, comforted by the intimacy and bliss. There is a deeper intimacy in the kitchen on Saturday when hair is pressed, when fish is fried, when sodas are passed around, when soul music drifts over the talk. We are women together. This is our ritual and our time. It is a time without men. It is a time when we work to meet each other's needs, to make each other beautiful in whatever way we can. It is a time of laughter and mellow talk. Sometimes it is an occasion for tears and sorrow. Mama is angry, sick of it all, pulling the hair too tight, using too much grease, burning one ear and then the next.

At first I cannot participate in the ritual. I have good

hair that does not need pressing. Without the hot comb I remain a child, one of the uninitiated. I plead, I beg, I cry for my turn. They tell me once you start you will be sorry. You will wish you had never straightened your hair. They do not understand that it is not the straightening I seek but the chance to belong, to be one in this world of women. It is finally my turn. I am happy. Happy even though my thin hair straightened looks like black thread, has no body, stands in the air like ends of barbed wire; happy even though the sweet smell of unpressed hair is gone forever. Secretly I had hoped that the hot comb would transform me, turn the thin good hair into thick nappy hair, the kind of hair I like and long for, the kind you can do anything with, wear in all kinds of styles. I am bitterly disappointed in the new look.

Later, a senior in high school, I want to wear a natural, an Afro. I want never to get my hair pressed again. It is no longer a rite of passage, a chance to be intimate in the world of women. The intimacy masks betrayal. Together we change ourselves. The closeness is an embrace before parting, a gesture of farewell to love and one another.

32

THERE IS A white discharge in my panties. It comes out of me like a leak, a tiny leak in a faucet that you hardly know is there except that a spot of water appears even after you have wiped it up in the same place. I am constantly wiping myself but the spots do not go away. I am constantly folding tissue to make perfect little napkins so that my panties will be clean, but the perfect little napkins wrinkle up, fall out when I am running. When mama finally asks me if it is me that has the panties with the discharge, with the sometimes funny smell, I do not ask her how she knows—she finds out everything. Yet she is mostly gentle when she comes across a secret that may hurt in the telling. I tell her I suppose they are mine. She wants to know have I been doing anything with boys. I do not know what this anything is. When I say no, she asks again and again. I always answer no. When I become tired of answering this same old question I ask her a question. I ask her What is this anything that one can do with boys. I am so angry at boys—the ones I do not know, who are capable of this anything that makes me be questioned in a way that feels like I have done something wrong, like I'm on trial. She does not want to tell me what the anything is. She believes me.

In the doctor's office she believes him when he says Yes sometimes young girls have these infections, no they are not caused by the anything that can be done with boys. I am to have a vinegar-and-water douche. I do not understand what it means. The sound of the word frightens me. They do not try and explain. They are annoyed that I am so ignorant when it comes to matters of the body. Yet they have always made us ashamed of the body, made us tuck it away under our pillows like some missing tooth for which the fairy will reward. They reward our silences about the body.

When mama is ready to give the douche she has me come into the bathroom and undress. Standing naked before her I pretend I am wearing clothes, that she cannot see the parts of me I have chosen to show to no one, the parts I no longer see myself even as I undress them, wash them. She looks at me as if she sees the clothes and not my nakedness. She is fully dressed. She explains to me that the vinegar and water are in the hot-water bottle, the red rubber thing that I had always thought of as a balloon that could never be blown up. When she tries to place the nozzle inside me, I know that I am naked, I know that this is my body, that she has no right to touch or enter. I begin to scream and scream—cries that sound as if a terrible crime is being committed. Worried that the neighbors will hear, she demands that I shut up before she kills me.

She needs an assistant. My oldest sister enters the bathroom with a smirk on her face that tells me right away that she sees that I am naked, afraid, ashamed; that she enjoys witnessing this humiliation. Together they struggle to perform the task. Mama asks angrily What are you going to do when some boy sticks his thing up you? I am shocked that she could think that I would ever be naked with a boy, that I would ever let anyone touch my body, or let them stick things in me. When I say this will never happen to me they stop their tasks to laugh, long and loud. I weep at their refusal to believe I can protect myself from further humiliation.

33

IT MAY HAVE been the pretend Tom Thumb wedding she had to participate in during first grade. It may have been that the tearing of her red crepe-paper bridesmaid dress convinced her she would fail at marriage just as she had failed at the pretend wedding. She knew that the pretend marriage had made her suspicious—nothing about it had been enjoyable. Whenever she thought of marriage she thought of it for someone else, someone who would make a beautiful bride, a good wife. From her perspective the problem with marriage was not the good wife, but the lack of the good husband. She is sixteen years old. Her mother is telling her again and again about the importance of learning to cook, clean, etc., in order to be a good wife. She stomps upstairs shouting, I will never be married! I will never marry! When she comes back downstairs she must explain why, she must find words—Seems like, she says, stammering, marriage is for men, that women get nothing out of it, men get everything. She did not want the mother to feel as if she was saying unkind things about her marriage. She did not want the mother to know that it was precisely her marriage that made it seem like a trap, a door closing in a room without air.

She could not tell her mother how she became a different person as soon as the husband left the house in the morning, how she became energetic, noisy, silly, funny, fussy, strong, capable, tender, everything that she was not when he was around. When he was around she became silent. She reminded her daughter of a dog sitting, standing obediently until the master, the head of the house, gave her orders to move, to do this to do that, to cook his food just so, to make sure the house was clean just so. Her bed was upstairs over their bedroom. She never heard them making fun sounds. She heard the plaintive pleading voice of the woman—she could not hear what she was asking for, begging for, but she knew that the schoolbooks, the bit of pocket money, the new dresses, the *everything* had to be paid for with more than money, with more than sex.

Whatever joy there was in marriage was something the women kept to themselves, a secret they did not share with one another or their daughters. She never asked where the joy was, when it appeared, why it had to be hidden. She was afraid of the answer. They agreed with her when she said marriage was not a part of her dreams. They said she was too thin, lacking the hips, breasts, thighs that men were interested in. But more importantly she was too smart, men did not like smart women, men did not like a woman whose head was always in a book. And even more importantly men did not like a woman who talked back. She had been hit, whipped, punished again and again for talking back. They had said they were determined to break her—to silence her, to turn her into one of them.

She answers her mother back one day in the father's presence. He slaps her hard enough to make her fall back, telling her Don't you ever let me hear you talking to your mother like that. She sees pride in the mother's face. She thinks about the ways he speaks to her, ways that at this moment do not matter. He has taken a stand in her honor against the daughter. She has accepted it. This, the daughter thinks, must be a kind of marriage—and she hopes never to bear a daughter to sacrifice in the name of such love.

34

WASH DAY IS a day of hard work. The machine is old and must be filled with water from buckets. Mama does most of the work. We love to stand and watch her put the clothes through the wringer after they are rinsed in huge tin buckets of water. They are the buckets we once took baths in when we were small children living on the hill. At night in the kitchen we would take turns being washed, washing. We think having our bodies washed by someone else's hands is one of the real pleasures of life. We have to grow older and bathe alone. We do—locking ourselves in to make sure no one joins us, witnesses the experience we were once more than willing to share. Everyone is irritable on wash day, especially in winter. The damp from the water and the cold enters our bones, chilling us. Clothes must be hung on the lines before we go to school. Our hands freeze as we hang piece after piece. Our feet feel the wet in the grass seeping through the thin soles of our shoes. Hanging piece after piece we move in slow motion hoping that we can go to school before the basket is empty. Mama warns us that we had better hang everything, that she does not care if we are late. In summer the clean clothes hanging in the fresh air are like rows of blossoming flowers. In winter they are like dead things frozen and cold. We bring the heavy work pants into the house frozen and stand them up in the bathtub where they will slowly thaw.

Washing means ironing. We come home from school knowing that the ironing board will stand ready, that the iron will be hot. Sometimes mama will still be ironing, her face hot, her feet hurting. We will stand and watch, telling her about our day. She will tell us who will begin ironing first. We learn to iron by pressing sheets. We do not know why sheets that are not even wrinkled must be ironed. Mama says it is practice. We especially hate ironing our father's underwear and pajamas. We especially hate being told that nothing was ironed correctly, that we must do the entire basket again.

It is my turn to iron. I can do nothing right. Before I begin I am being yelled at. I hear again and again that I am crazy, that I will end up in a mental institution. This is my punishment for wanting to finish reading before doing my work, for taking too long to walk down the stairs. Mama is already threatening to smack me if I do not stop rolling my eyes and wipe that frown off my face. It is times like these that I am sorry to be alive, that I want to die. In the kitchen with my sisters, she talks on and on about how she cannot stand me, about how I will go crazy. I am warned that if I begin to cry I will be given something to cry about. The tears do not fall. They stand in my eyes like puddles. They keep me from seeing where the ironing is going. I want them to shut up. I want them to leave me alone. I shout at them Leave Me Alone! I sit the hot iron on my arm. Already someone is laughing and yelling about what the crazy fool has done to herself. Already I have begun to feel the pain of the burning flesh. They do not stop talking. They say no one will visit me in the mental hospital. Mama says it does not matter about the pain, I must finish ironing the clothes in my basket.

35

MISS RHOBERT LIVES around the corner in one of the storybook houses—white white with green grass, red brick steps, and matching porch furniture. Of course she never sits on the porch as that is the kind of thing the common folk do. She is not common. She comes from a long line of folks who look white. When we were small children we thought they were the color of pigs in storybooks. We know now that they are the black landowners, business people. We know now that they stand between white folks and real black folks. Like gossip, white folks spread their messages to us through them. They hate both white folks and dark black people. They hate white folks for having what they want. They hate dark black folks for reminding the world that they are colored and thus keeping them from really getting what they want. They never pass for white. They do not want to live in white communities and be treated like second-class citizens, like poor white folks are treated. They want to live in the heart of black communities where they will be looked up to, envied, where their every move will be talked about.

Miss Rhobert is one of them. She is unmarried and getting on in age. She will never marry because no one is good enough they say. She will never marry because no one has asked her they say. She was my first grade teacher. She lives alone. She has divided her house into two flats. She lives in one. Her roomers, all single men, live in the other. They live together without really seeing one another. They may not bring their women to stay. When they are gone she must look elsewhere for comfort, protection, for knowledge that she is not alone. She suggests to my mother that I should come stay nights with her, that in exchange she will give a few dollars a week and sometimes help with the buying of schoolbooks. Going to her house after dinner is a way to avoid conflict. She and I have little to say to one another. We will eat candy or ice cream, watch TV, and go to bed. I must sleep in the same bed with her. I hide myself in the corner of the bed near the wall and pretend I am not there. She sleeps soundly, snoring, her mouth open. When she pays me I will hand the money to mama who will determine what I need, how it will be spent. The money brings me no pleasure. I am never free to choose what to buy. When I assert my right to choose she never lets me forget.

Nights at Miss Rhobert's I learn the art of being present and not present at the same time. It is the art of being a good servant. It is knowing what it is to stay in one's place. I do not speak unless I am spoken to. I do not converse, I answer back in short sentences. When I laugh it sounds as though I am afraid. Sometimes I bring a book to read. This sign that I am not always a servant, not always in my place, leads her to make conversation. She wants to know what is being talked about at my house, who is doing what. I learn the art of avoiding answering her questions directly. When we are not watching television we play Scrabble. She likes to play for money. I do not as I am afraid to win. Since she has never learned to drive a car Miss Rhobert cannot go out at night unless someone comes for her. Sometimes, every now and then, she leaves me alone for a few minutes. The muscles in my body relax, I am no longer invisible in my chair. I am grateful for the silence. Mama decides for me that I am too old for this job. My younger sister takes my place.

36

WHEN WE FIRST meet I am shy. She reminds me of the small brown bird I held in my hand days ago. We were in the backyard playing when we saw the bird on the fence. It seemed to be waiting for me. When I held it in my hand I could feel the quivering, the heartbeat. It was so alive and so delicate that I felt responsible and afraid. I put it back on the fence and waited until it flew away. To me she is that bird given human form. Miss Willie Gray is a brown-skinned woman with gray hair. She is in her nineties. She is afflicted with palsy. These are her words: Affliction makes me think of church and the Bible. She moves her arms as though they are wings continually flapping. She has learned to anticipate the trembling movement—to see it as a sign that she is still alive. The movements do not bother me. They remind me of the bird flying away. She wants to fly and cannot. We both agree that it is not a sad thing for she is able to be independent, to move around, to cook for herself, to plant a garden. She is alone, old, and happy. She tells me always, Who could ask for anything more.

They say she never married because she was too attached to her father. I believe them because she talks to me endlessly about him. She tells me how he bought the grocery store and let her work in it even though it was not considered the proper thing for a lady to do. She told me how he died and left the store to her along with money and land. She tells me that she would have given all those things away if only he could have remained alive. Her mother had died when they were still girls. She took over the running of the house. In those days she said it was a common thing for the eldest daughter to housekeep until a new wife could be found. Her father never found a new wife though he had women. She stayed to housekeep and care for him until he died. She never wanted to marry. She fascinates me because all the other independent unmarried women are schoolteachers who began work in those days when the law required them to remain single. She never tires of telling me that it is her choice to remain single and alone.

She is not always alone. I am hired to come and stay nights, to do chores in the day, to go to the store now and then. At her house I have my own bed. I can read all night long and books are in every room. We both love to lie in bed and read. She reads *True Confessions*. Although I buy them at the store I do not read them. She has a copy of Milton's *Paradise Lost* which I read again and again. Her books are all hardback. They are mainly popular novels. She no longer reads them. She tells me I can read them whenever I want. We are good company for each other. Now and then I must leave my bed to get water or medicine for her. She never goes anywhere. She stays in her yard and in her garden. She loves to walk up and down the rows of growing things. I tell her that I did this all the time when I was younger. Now I sit on the fence and watch.

They would like to put her in a home, a place where they would not have to worry about her. They say that they are worried that she might fall down and hurt herself. She says they want her house, her money. She intends to stay in her house alone until she dies. She tells me that to leave her house and go to an old folk's home would be the end. In a harsh voice she wants me to tell her why they cannot leave her in peace. I remain silent, listening, watching the flapping wings.

37

HER BROTHER'S ROOM has become her room. He has
become a man and gone away to do what men do—to be a
soldier. A dark room with no windows, cold in winter, cool
in summer, it is her place of refuge and recovery. The
tensions of high school, family, friendship can all be re-
leased there. She can hide from the loneliness inside. She
can pretend. She can read all night long. To them she is the
problem child, the source of all their pain. Everyone else
gets along well together. She is the one who is no fun, who
makes trouble. Before he goes she and her five sisters share
upstairs rooms—six girls in two rooms. Four in the front
room and two in the back. For years her first bed is just as
you come up the stairs. Beds are placed in strange ways in
the room because the ceilings slope like an attic. It is near a
window that reaches from low ceiling to the floor. All

night she can gaze out watching the stars, watching the lights in the neighbor's windows, watching birds, watching rain. It is her only private space. All her favorite things live there with her—books, paintbrushes, diaries.

She is not very tidy. Her corner, like all the other spaces in the room, is crammed full with things. When her mother sweeps under the bed they are all outraged, embarrassed. These upstairs rooms are painted pink. She hates the color pink. Grown-ups think it should be her favorite color. Pink innocence, pink dreams, pink the color of something alive but not quite allowed to be fully living. She liked deep reds, black, dark greens. They would never let the rooms be painted another color. All girls want a pink room—she and her sisters should be content, happy to live in a world of pink. To her younger sisters, she is the one who is different. They cannot sleep at night because she is always crying. They demand that their mother make her stop crying. She learns to hold her tears, to keep them silent until everyone is sound asleep and the house is still. She cries about not being able to do anything right, about not fitting in, about being unfairly punished, about being punished.

When an older sister leaves home she is first moved to the back room, sharing it. Her younger sisters are glad to see her go. She is not at home in her new space. It can never be truly hers, so completely did it bear the mark of the oldest sister. In that room her secrets are always found. Her diaries are read, her hidden money stolen, her clothes disappearing. Everything that is private someone will find and hang on the line like wet clothes for everyone to see. They love the pain it causes her. They resent her for needing so badly to shut them out. In this room she hardly ever cries. She stays awake nights talking to god, trying to find this stranger that will understand, that will make everything right. Perhaps she cries less because all the sounds made in this room can be heard by her parents lying in their bed underneath. There are no more problems with her keeping the lights on—her older sister, when she is home, does not care. Once she falls asleep nothing and no one disturbs her. Anyway, the space belonged to her oldest sister. It was her things that were everywhere; she invaded other people's things and made them her own.

Finally mama decides she should move downstairs. They give her the boy's room, not because she is the oldest of the youngest, not because she is deserving, but because she is the problem, the one no one can stand. She is to live in exile. They are glad to see her go, they feel as if something had died that they had long waited to be rid of but were not free to throw away. Like in church, they excommunicate her.

38

MASTURBATION IS SOMETHING she has never heard
anyone talk about girls doing. Like so many spaces of fun
and privilege in their world, it is reserved for the boy
child—the one whose growing passion for sexuality can be
celebrated, talked about with smiles of triumph and pleasure. A boy coming into awareness of his sexuality is on his
way to manhood—it is an important moment. The stained
sheets that show signs of his having touched his body are
flags of victory. They—the girls—have no such moments.
Sexuality is something that will be done to them, something they have to fear. It can bring unwanted pregnancy.
It can turn one into a whore. It is a curse. It will ruin a
young girl's life, pull her into pain again and again, into
childbirth, into welfare, into all sorts of longings that will
never be satisfied. Again and again they tell their mother

she does not need to worry about them. They are not sexual. They will not get pregnant, will not bring home babies for her to take care of. They do not actually say We are not sexual for the very use of the word *sexual* might suggest knowledge—they make sexuality synonymous with pregnancy, with being a whore, a slut.

When she finds pleasure touching her body, she knows that they will think it wrong; that it is something to keep hidden, to do in secret. She is ashamed, ashamed that she comes home from school wanting to lie in bed touching the wet dark hidden parts of her body, ashamed that she lies awake nights touching herself, moving her hands, her fingers deeper and deeper inside, inside the place of woman's pain and misery, the place men want to enter, the place babies come through—ashamed of the pleasure.

When she finally has a room all to herself she can go there when no one notices and enjoy her body. This pleasure is her secret and her shame. She denies to herself that she is being sexual. She refuses to think about it. Males are not the object of her lust. She does not touch herself thinking about their penises moving inside her, the wetness of their ejaculations. It is her own wetness that the fingers seek. It is the moment she thinks of, not as orgasm, for she does not know the word, but as the moment of climbing a tall place and reaching the top. This is what she longs for. There she finds a certain contentedness and bliss. It is this bliss the fingers guide her to. Like the caves she dreamed about in childhood it is a place of refuge, a sanctuary.

Like all secret pleasure she finds the hiding hard. She knows her sisters have begun to wonder about the moments alone in the dark cool room, the times in bed reading when they are outside. They watch her, waiting. They open the door fast. They pull the covers quickly before she can free her hands. They bear witness to her pleasure and her shame. Her pleasure in the body, her shame at being found out. They threaten to tell, they can't wait to tell. She prepares her denial. She goes over and over it in her head. Like a party ending because the lights are suddenly turned on she knows the secret moments are gone, the dark, the pleasure, the deep cool ecstasy.

39

NO ONE EVER talks to her about playing with herself,
touching her body, about masturbation. She does not
know if they told her mother. No one says anything. She is
on guard, she is the watcher. She no longer touches herself.
She does not like to mingle pleasure with fear. She does
not like the smell of fear. She reads with passion and intensity. When she has read everything in sight she goes searching for something new, something undiscovered. Books,
like hands in the dark place, are a source of pleasure. In her
search for new reading she finds books kept in her father's
private space, kept behind his bed. She has never heard
the word pornography. To her they are just books with
funny covers. The people on the covers do not look real.
They are all white women, wearing heavy makeup, tight
red dresses revealing body parts, they are naked. She does

not know that these books are not to be read. She hides her reading of them solely because they can be punished for taking things from his private space.

In bed with her new reading she finds that the books are about kinds of sex, not the sex married, religious people have, but the dirty kind, the kind people have for pleasure. Excited by the reading, by the coming together of these two pleasures, books and sex, she learns that sex does not take place solely between men and women. Sex takes place between women and women, men and men, women and men in groups. Sex takes place with people watching—with people masturbating. Sometimes people like doing things with the sex she thinks are strange, whipping, eating, swimming. She finds that while reading these books her body is aroused, she feels the mounting wetness in her panties. She had thought the wetness came with the hand movement. This new discovery surprises her. It makes the touching more exciting, bringing images and fantasies to what was once just a good, warm wet feeling. Sex in these new books fascinates her. There are no babies to be had through the excitement these pages arouse, no pain, no male abuse, no abandonment. She never thinks much about the roles women and men play in the books. They have no relationship to real people. The men do not work, the women do not have children, clean house, go shopping. Sometimes the men make the women do sexual acts. She could never understand how the women did what they didn't want to do, yet felt pleasure in doing it. She never felt pleasure doing what she did not want to do.

It becomes harder and harder for her to take the books. She must wait until no one is watching. She must make sure she puts them back exactly as she finds them. She is caught, creeping up the stairs with a book in hand. Her mother does not want to see the book, only for her to put it back where she found it, only for her to stop reading them. It is her favorite book, *Passion Pit*. It is the only book wherein she identifies with a woman in the one part where the man uses his tongue and fingers to sexually arouse his partner, then withdraws, telling her if she wants sex to ask for it, telling her to beg for it, to want it enough to beg. She can understand the intensity of the woman's longing, her willingness to ask, possibly even to beg. She knows this affirmation of the woman's sexual hunger is exactly what would be denied her in real life. Long after the books are all destroyed she recalls the image of the sexually hungry woman wanting it, wanting it enough to ask, even to beg.

40

DIRTY BOOKS SHE could read but not *True Confessions,*
not *Sepia,* not any of those magazines with their endless
sad stories of sex gone wrong. Women in those pages were
always guilty, were always begging pardon. When she
stopped reading dirty books because her father no longer
kept them around the house, because the ones she had
managed to get for herself no longer interested her, she
started reading the stuff recommended by the older white
woman at the library. She read George Eliot, Henry James,
Emily Brontë, Charlotte Brontë. Like so many places in
the white folk's world she knew they considered her presence at the library an intrusion. They watched her suspi-
ciously. When she checked out books they turned them
over and over in their hands, as if the books were hiding
some secret, as if they needed to understand why this

black girl was reading this or that. She tried waiting always for the one friendly one, the one who did not treat her like dirt, who did not ask her Are you sure you can read all these books?

When she began reading popular romances from the early 1900s she would spend hours searching the shelves for something new, something she had not read. Her favorite was *Lena Rivers,* a story of a poor southern white girl raised by her grandmother who moves north only to discover her real father is a rich gentleman, only to fall in love with and marry his son. Of course this simple story did not take place without incredible mishap, intrigue, mystery. She liked the mystery as much as the romance. To escape the library she gave herself over to reading popular paperback romances. She read only one kind, the Mills & Boon that will later become Harlequin romances. She liked them best because they were updated versions of *Lena Rivers.* The woman was almost always poor, a working woman, almost always missing physical beauty by some slight flaw, hair that was too red, too short, too thin, long nose, poor eyesight. What beauty they possessed was always an inner quality, unfolding, blossoming when the right man came along. These women were always in need of rescue despite their independence, their work ability. They always loved children. They would abandon work, travel thousands of miles to strange countries, to care for children. They were always virgins. They always married. Their stories always had happy endings.

It was the knowledge that everything would come right in the end that made these romances the only ones she would ever read. It was important to her to know just how the book would end, that everything would turn out just right. It was important to her because she did not live a life where everything turned out all right, where women or men were rescued. She saw women and men all around in distress, feeling pain, waiting for the rescue that never came. She saw herself as one of them. She was one of those children who had come to believe that it was somehow all a mistake that she had been born into this family, into this life of never being able to do anything right, of endless torment. Romance fiction gave her escape, release, a feeling of satisfaction, a belief in the possibility of self-recovery.

They were glad to see her cease reading those mysterious hardback books that were difficult for them to read and understand. They were glad to witness her addiction to romance. They began to see her as more normal. They had warned her that books could drive people crazy. They had warned that living her life she would truly end up crazy, locked up, alone. They had told her that there would never be any rescue.

41

THE HOUSE ON First Street has a downstairs bedroom
we call the middle room. It is between our parents' bedroom and the boy's room. We only sleep in the middle
room when we are sick. We sleep there so mama does not
have to run up and down the stairs waiting on us. From
the middle room she can hear us calling her name from the
kitchen, she can hear us crying because we feel bad. During my late-night asthma attacks I sleep there, when I can
sleep. The curtains in that room are blue and white, they
have a poem on them, a sonnet that ends with the line I
shall but love thee better after death. In school I learn that
this is one of the most famous poems from Elizabeth Bar-
rett Browning's collection, *Sonnets from the Portuguese.*
Memorizing it I repeat it daily—until everyone is tired of
hearing it. We think these curtains should be in the middle

room because the sick and the dying lie here. We think we cannot bear to lose anyone we love to death. We like to pretend that only old people die but we know it is not so.

We know it is not so because Zinn, a little girl who played piano, fell in the lake on our Sunday school picnic and drowned. We cannot understand the dying away of young things. We understand the unending grief of her mother, because we, too, cannot believe she is really gone. Then there is the death of one of our brother's high school friends. He is so beautiful with his light brown skin and curly hair that girls go wild over him. Because he is sometimes sick, sick with fits, with epilepsy, he is all the more popular, all the more loved. We are so accustomed to seeing him, to having him and our brother's other friend eating us out of house and home that we find it hard to accept his death, to think of him as gone. We are not allowed to attend the funeral, only my brother who, with his other friends will carry the casket. The service takes place in a little church. It is not a Baptist church. So many people attend the funeral that some must stand outside. The funeral sermon can hardly be heard over the crying sound of the girls whose hearts he has touched. They faint and are carried from the church while the family remains to moan, to mourn the loss.

We bring our dying to the middle room. When Big Mama is sick she comes to lie there, to be waited on by mama. They talk about whether or not to send her to the hospital. Old people are not sent to the hospital if they are sick enough to die. They say that there is no point, that somebody who can get well may need the hospital bed. They do not talk about the money that is saved—they know that often for the old there is no money. When Big Mama's sickness worsens the doctor comes. He talks in a low voice to mama. We know what is being said. We know he is telling her that it will not be long, that there is no hope, that she must just make her comfortable. Little washbasins are continually filled with blood and taken from the room to be emptied. This death is different from the one I witnessed as a young girl. Here there is the lingering smell of fresh blood. Like a hunting dog chasing its prey, death enters. There is a desperation in the bodies as they move in and out of the room. Without asking I run outside. I run from the smell into the moist summer air.

42

WHEN THEY RETURN from the funeral all they can talk about is the way the mama let that child wear a black dress. Black is a woman's color. They know better. Now a dark navy blue dress, even brown, are the right colors for children. Her mama feels that children do not even belong at funerals, that is, unless they are real close to the dead person. We do not get a chance to go to our father's mother's funeral. Before mama can tell us it is discovered that we all have measles. Death and measles at the same time. It makes her very tired. She does not even mention to their tired mama that she has already planned her black dress, the one she will wear to mourn. To her, black is not a mourning color. Death is not a mourning time. She is disappointed that they cannot go to a funeral. She grows older, never wanting to go to funerals. They go instead to view the body—entering the funeral home silently with their fat sympathy cards. They take in every detail so as to be able to join in the discussion of how the dead look. She cannot understand the importance of knowing whether or not the dead look well. Most importantly they want to know if the dead body resembles the living being. A well-laid-out body is one that looks just as if the person is asleep. That was the way her aunt looked, the one that died young, that died in childbirth. All the pictures of her lying still in the casket looked like pictures of sleeping, contented, well-fed babies. She never understood why having a baby could kill you. They never explained. Death was the unexplainable. Sickness they could talk about for days, but not death. Silence surrounds death and dying.

She is almost a senior in high school before she goes to her first funeral. When the elderly woman that she stays with at night dies the grown-ups consider it only proper that she go to pay her respects. Her feelings are mixed. She wants to witness this public treatment of death and yet she is somehow afraid that it might touch her deeply, in some irreparable way. She is not allowed to wear a black dress. She wears instead a favorite navy blue and gray pin-striped skirt with matching vest and a white blouse. She goes with her sister Valeria. They whisper together before the services begin, telling each other that it is like being at a movie theater. She keeps thinking this through the whole sermon. It is all major drama.

The remaining family there grieving had never had the

time to come sit and visit. They were always busy, always unable to make it even after she made the regular phone calls suggesting that it would be a good thing if they stopped by. She made the phone calls as part of her job. She answered the calls that were always wrong numbers. This same family sat at the front of the church weeping, holding handkerchiefs to their faces, holding on to one another. Their bodies shook with grief as they walked by the dead old lady whose gray hair they had the undertaker dye black. She is no different. She, too, is an imposter at the funeral. She cannot mourn this passing because the life had been long, full, and satisfying. She cannot really feel sad even though she wants to. She fears only one moment—that moment when it is her turn to walk by the body, to stand there still and grieving. When their row walks past the casket she refuses to look directly at the body. She only glanced at death. It makes her want to laugh and cry at the same time. She covers her mouth with her hands.

43

JAZZ, SHE LEARNS from her father, is the black man's music, the working man, the poor man, the man on the street. Different from the blues because it does not simply lament, moan, express sorrow, it expresses everything. She listens to a record he is playing, to a record that is being played on the radio. It is the music of John Coltrane. Her father says this is a musician who understands all the black man is longing for, that he takes this longing and blows it out of his saxophone. Like the alchemist he turns lead into gold. To listen, he tells her, is to feel understood. She listens, wanting this jazz not to be beyond her, wanting it to address the melancholy parts of her soul. To her, black people make the most passionate music. She knows that there is no such thing as natural rhythm. She knows it is the intensity of feeling, the constant knowing that death is real and a possibility that makes the music what it is. She knows that it is the transformation of suffering and sorrow into sound that bears witness to a black past. In her dreams she has seen the alchemist turning lead into gold.

On communion Sundays they sing without musical accompaniment. They keep alive the old ways, the call and response. They sing slow and hold each note as if it is caught in the trap of time—struggling to be free. Like the bread and the wine they do it this way so as to not forget what the past has been. She listens to the strength in the voices of elderly women as they call out. She sings in the choir. She loves the singing. She looks forward to choir practice on Wednesday night. It is the only weekday night that they are away from home. They sit in the basement of the church singing. They sing, Hush children, hush children, somebody's calling my name, oh, my lord, oh, my lordy, what shall I do.

At home her mama listens to music. On Friday nights she sits in her corner on the couch, smoking one cigarette, drinking one can of beer, playing records, staring sadly into the smoke as Brook Benton sings, You don't miss your water till your well runs dry. Saturday morning they clean house and listen to music. They listen to the soul music on the radio. It is the only time they can hear a whole program with black music. Every other day is country and western or rock 'n' roll. In between vacuuming, dusting, and sweeping they listen to the latest songs and show each other the latest dances. Even though she likes to dance, she is not a good dancer. Awkward, unable to keep in step, they make fun of her. She cannot slow dance. She does not know how to follow the lead. She gives up dancing, spends her time listening to the music.

She likes the music of Louis Armstrong. She likes to see the pleasure he brings to her father's face. They watch him on the *Ed Sullivan Show,* making funny faces, singing in his deep voice. It is the trumpet sound that they are waiting for. When he pulls the handkerchief from his pocket to wipe away the dripping sweat she is reminded of the right-hand men of god weeping into thin squares of cotton. She imagines tears mingled with Satchmo's sweat, that they are tears of gratitude, that he, too, is giving thanks for finding in his horn yet another sweet-stretching sound he did not know was there.

44

SHE WANTS TO express herself—to speak her mind. To them it is just talking back. Each time she opens her mouth she risks punishment. They punish her so often she feels they persecute her. When she learns the word *scapegoat* in vocabulary lesson, she is sure it accurately describes her lot in life. Her wilderness, unlike the one the goat is led into, is a wilderness of spirit. They abandon her there to get on with the fun things of life. She lies in her bed upstairs after being punished yet again. She can hear the sound of their laughter, their talk. No one hears her crying. Even though she is young she comes to understand the meaning of exile and loss. They say that she is really not a young girl but an old woman born again in a young girl's body. They do not know how to speak the old woman's language so they are afraid of her. She might be a witch. They have given her a large thick paperback of original fairy tales. On page after page an old woman is eating children, thinking some wicked deed, performing evil magic. She is not surprised that they fear the old woman inside her. A lover of old women, she understands that the old women in the fairy tales do evil because they are misunderstood. She does not mind at all when they look at her and say She must be ninety, look at the way she walks. No! they say, She must be at least a hundred. Only a hundred-year-old woman could walk so slow.

Their world is the only world there is. To be exiled from it is to be without life. She cries because she is in mourning. They will not let her wear the color black. It is not a color for girls. To them she already looks too old. She would just look like a damn fool in a black dress. Black is a woman's color.

She finds another world in books. Escaping into the world of novels is one way she learns to enjoy life. But novels only ease the pain momentarily, as she holds the book in hand, as she reads. It is poetry that changes everything. When she discovers the Romantics it is like losing a part of herself and recovering it. She reads them night and day, all the time. She memorizes poems. She recites them ironing or washing dishes. Reading Emily Dickinson she senses that the spirit can grow in the solitary life. She reads Edna St. Vincent Millay's "Renascence," feels with the lines the suppression of spirit, the spiritual death, and the longing to live again. She reads Whitman, Wordsworth, Coleridge.

Whitman shows her that language, like the human spirit, need not be trapped in conventional form or traditions. For school she recites "O Captain, My Captain." She would rather recite from *Song of Myself* but they do not read it in school. They do not read it because it would be hard to understand. She cannot understand why everyone hates to read poetry. She cannot understand their moans and groans. She wishes they did not have to recite poems. She cannot bear to hear afraid voices stumbling through lines as if they are a wilderness and a trap. At home she practices reciting with everyone watching.

She writes her own poetry in secret. She does not want to explain. Her poems are about love and never about death. She is always thinking about death and never about love. She knows that they will think it better to discover secret poems about love. She knows they never speak of death. The punishments continue. She eases her pain in poetry, using it to make the poems live, using the poems to keep on living.

45

AS PART OF our missionary work we go to sing spirituals in the mental hospital. We go to play with the children who are there. We must be careful when we play, careful not to be bitten, careful not to fight. When we enter we go through door after door; each is locked behind us. Each door opens into a room that smells to me more and more like dying. I feel that I cannot breathe. I cannot understand the rooms without air, without windows. I cannot understand the darkness in the daytime. I cannot bear the institutional coldness. I am glad that I have brought a sweater. Inside we try to make everyone happy, especially the children. We dance with them. We dance until we are so tired, so drained. We dance until our hearts are full— always on the way home we are silent in the bus, in the car. We know that it is not life to be locked in, without air. We know that it is a slow and quiet torture. We cannot see how anyone will be made well.

Some of the people there, the children (they are mainly women and children), seem to be only a little strange, seem to have a little physical handicap. To us it is only a little strange to talk to yourself, or sing to yourself constantly, but not strange enough to be locked away. We do not see why anyone who moves ever so slow, like a turtle, like a sick car, like an animal stalking its prey, must be locked up. We do not understand and we do not ask questions. When they close each door and turn the lock I feel something inside me grow afraid. I feel my blood turn into a cold despair traveling through my entire body and I shiver. I wonder if those who stay, who never leave, learn to close their ears to the sound of the doors, the turning locks. Even if I could learn to not hear the locks I am sure the smell would kill me, would take my life slowly, stealing a bit of it each day with everyone watching. Nearly all the people locked in are white. At home they tell us white folks do not want black people in their mental institutions. Private places cost money, black people do not have money to pay for the sick. Anyhow, they say most people do not need to be locked up. They laugh and say they lock up all the wrong people, that some of those people locked up are too crazy to harm a fly and all the normal folk walking around killing and hurting one another.

In our neighborhoods there are people walking around that they would maybe lock up. We call the one who cannot

134

talk, whose mouth never closes, Slobber Boy. We see him always walking to the store buying candy, walking alone on the railroad tracks. We do not know where he lives but he has a home and people. They see to his needs. When we talk to him he smiles at us. Sometimes children, even some of us, make fun of him. We know better. Then there is the Hook-Arm Man. We have heard that he sticks his hook into children and cooks them over an open fire. We know to stay away from him but we near his house anyway. We see him on the porch. He seems like any old man alone. They say he is not always good to children so we stay away. They do not say Lock him up. They say He really hurts no one. Then there is the woman in a distant relative's house—her daughter, the one born crazy, the one that never grew up. Then there is Miss Beulah whose body never stopped growing, whose teeth and toenails are like fangs. I sit with her a few times each week to read, to talk. She has trouble talking. She may be crazy but there is no need to put her away, to lock her up. Sometimes she walks in the backyard, or sits on the porch. It is better than being locked up. It is better they say to keep in touch with these wounded parts of our selves. In some way they are us.

46

WHEN THEY TALK about same-sex love they use the word *funny*. They never say the word *homosexual*. As small children we think to be called funny is a nice way of talking about something grown-ups are uncertain about, ashamed and even a bit afraid of. Growing older we learn to be afraid of being called funny because it can change everything. Mostly men we know are funny. Everyone knows who they are and everyone watches and talks about their business. They are good men, kind men, respected men in the community and it is not their fault, not their choice that they are funny—they are just that way. They had to accept themselves and we had to accept them. We do not make fun of them. We know better.

Funny men are different from other men because they want secretly to be able to do the things that women do.

They want to care about people, about how they dress themselves, about how the inside of their houses look, about the food they eat. They do not need women in their lives to care about these things for them the way men with wives and girlfriends do. They are only interested in talking to women. Fascinated by their lives, grown-ups watch them as if they were at a circus watching something incredible. Sometimes when a new male, a young male, joins the group that gathers at certain houses, the community blames it on his mother. They talk about how she made him learn to cook, to clean, to take care of small children— all the things that real men should never learn. We don't like real men. We don't like the way our brother never has to iron, wash dishes, or take care of babies. We don't like the contempt he seems to feel for us girls as he watches us doing those things, as he sweet-talks us into doing his chores, mopping the floor, putting out the trash. Since he shows all the right interest in girls mama does not mind his going around the men who are funny as long as he does not go too often, does not make a habit of it.

When I go to one of the houses where homosexual men are sitting around drinking and talking to one another, I feel as though I am entering a world that does not concern me. I feel as though I am being forced to peer through a keyhole to look at something I am not interested in seeing. I want so much to have more privacy in my life. I do not want to enter the privacy of others. I stand on the porch not wanting to follow my friend inside, not wanting to admit that I am afraid of the huge barking dog that comes to the door to announce our presence. I have come with a friend. It is the house of her relative. She comes often. When the men talk to me I answer back shyly. I do not want to look them in the eye because I do not want to be staring. I want to know nothing so that I can answer no questions.

When grown-ups talk about women who are funny, they are not accepting. Their voices are harsh and unforgiving. They do not see them as kind, respected, *good* women. They talk about them as unnatural, strange, going against god. I want so badly to know why these women must live secretly, must sometimes be married. It is hard to ask questions. When I do they let me know quickly that men have the right to do whatever they want to do and that women must always follow rules. Rules like women are made to have babies. Only by being with men can women have babies. Women who do not want to be with men must be made to feel bad, ashamed, must be excluded from all community of feeling so that they will come to do what is expected of them—if not, they will be punished, they will be alone—they will not be loved.

47

I AM MOST passionate in my relationship with mama. It is with her that I feel loved and sometimes accepted. She is the one person who looks into my heart, sees its needs and tries to satisfy them. She is also always trying to make me be what she thinks is best for me to be. She tells me how to do my hair, what clothes I should wear. She wants to love and control at the same time. Her love is sustained and deep. Sometimes I feel like a drowning person saved by the pulling and tugging, saved by the breath of air that is her caring. I want to tell her this but the gifts we buy on Mother's Day, at Christmas, on birthdays seem only to make a mockery of that love, to suggest that it is something cheap and silly, something that is not needed. I do not want to give these gifts. I do not want to take these times to show my care, times someone else has chosen. She interprets my silence, my last-minute effort at a gift, as a sign of the way I am an uncaring girl. The fact that I disappoint her leaves me lying awake at night sobbing, wanting to be a better daughter, a daughter that makes her life brighter, easier. I am a pain to her. She says that she is not sure where I come from, that she would like to send me back. I want so much to please her and yet keep some part of me that is myself, my own, not just a thing I have been turned into that she can desire, like, or do with as she will. I want her to love me totally as I am. I love her totally without wanting that she change anything, not even the things about her that I cannot stand.

Whenever I try to speak to her about the things that weigh deeply on my heart, that press it down like a stone, crushing it, she changes the subject. I think it is because she cannot bear to hear about a pain that she cannot understand, that she cannot make better. She has no time for pain. There is so much work for her to do. When I use the word lonely she does not say anything. She closes her ears. It is as if the second pair of hands, the pair she stows away in pockets, closets, and drawers to get all the work done that there is no time to do, those invisible hands cover her ears. She does not want to hear the word *loneliness.* She does not want to remember. I tell her that I want to die before her, that I cannot live without her. This makes her angry. She thinks these are too-strange words for a daughter to say. She tells me to shut up saying foolish things. She tells me that of course she will die before me, that she is older. She says such thoughts will drive me crazy, that I should be outside playing, outside being young and happy. I am sure passion disturbs her. She reads women's magazines. I am sure that they do not tell her what to do with a child that thinks about dying, that knows the specialness, the unique beauty of her care.

We can tell that our mama is not like other mothers. We can see that she is working hard to give us more than food, shelter, and clothes to wear, that she wants to give us a taste of the delicious, a vision of beauty, a bit of ecstasy. Even so, she is obsessed with the latest products. Even so, she is moving away from her awareness of the deeper inner things of life and worrying more about money. I watch these changes in her and worry. I want her never to lose what she has given me—a sense that there is something deeper, something more to this life than the everyday.

48

WHEN SHE SPEAKS of dying I do not want to listen.
I do not want to ever imagine a world in which she is not.
She tells us that we must know the possibility that is her
death. She tells us where everything important is. She tells
us about the clothes she would like to be buried in, about
where in her chest of drawers we can find things. She
wants to make us close to one another—a family that can
go off even if she is no longer with us. We are not sure
what all this talk of death means. We know it must mean
something. She tells us finally that she is very sick, that she
must go into the hospital and have a serious operation. We
know that it is serious because she does not go to the black
hospital but across town, to the one we cannot walk to,
where we know no one. When we want to know what is
wrong, what is really wrong she does not say. This is one of
her ways that I cannot stand. Thinking to protect us she

makes us very afraid, so afraid we are silent. Words like cancer, tumor, hang suspended in the air like rain in dark clouds waiting to soak us at any moment. It is the uncertainty that makes me hide in books. She sees it as another sign that I am uncaring, without feeling, hateful. I see the invisible hands cover her eyes so that she does not have to see our fear. Since she cannot say There is nothing to worry about, do not be afraid, she refuses to acknowledge our fear.

She does not think about being sick. She is busy planning. Shopping for the food, planning the meals, making lists, tiring herself out. She has no space during the day to be afraid. I lie awake nights listening, wondering if she is lying in the dark crying, wondering if she is clutching his body trying to ward off the coldness of death. I hear nothing but the sound of her footsteps as she walks from the front of the house to the back, finishing some chore she cannot leave until the morning. We want to know if we will be able to visit her in the hospital. It is then that we see the fear in her lips, the trembling, the hesitation. Again she wants to protect us, again she is hiding. I walk away. I cannot stand the hiding. I cannot stand all the secret places I have had to make inside myself. No one comes to stay with us, not like the old days. We are big. We are able to follow orders. We fear punishment if we disobey. To come home from school and find her not there is already a hint of loss. We feel the emptiness, the cold place that her heart warms. We go room to room to see if everything is still there in place.

They say she is near death, that we must go and see her because it may be the last time. I will not go. I have my own ideas about death. I see her all the time. I see her as she moves about the house doing things, cooking, cleaning, fussing. I refuse to go. I cannot tell them why, that I do not want to have the last sight of her be there in the white hospital bed, surrounded by strangers and the smell of death. She does not die. She comes home angry, not wanting to see the uncaring daughter, the one who would not even come to say good-bye. She is in control. She is not yet ready to love. She does not understand. Upstairs in my hiding place I cry. They tell her She is upstairs crying and will not stop. She sends me orders to stop crying right this minute, that I have nothing to cry about, that she should be crying to have such a terrible daughter. When I go to her, sitting on the bed, with my longing and my tears she knows that she breaks my heart a little. She thinks I break her heart a little. She cannot know the joy we feel that she is home, alive.

49

THEY HAVE NEVER heard their mama and daddy fussing or fighting. They have heard him be harsh, complain that the house should be cleaner, that he should not have to come home from work to a house that is not cleaned just right. They know he gets mad. When he gets mad about the house he begins to clean it himself to show that he can do better. Although he never cooks he knows how. He would not be able to judge her cooking if he did not cook himself. They are afraid of him when he is mad. They go upstairs to get out of his way. He does not come upstairs. Taking care of children is not a man's work. It does not concern him. He is not even interested—that is, unless something goes wrong. Then he can show her that she is not very good at parenting. They know they have a good mama, the best. Even though they fear him they are not moved by his opinions. She tries to remember a time when she felt loved by him. She remembers it as being the time when she was a baby girl, a small girl. She remembers him taking her places, taking her to the world inhabited by black men, the barbershop, the pool hall. He took his affections away from her abruptly. She never understood why, only that they went and did not come back. She remembered trying to do whatever she could to bring them back, only they never came. Growing up she stopped trying. He mainly ignored her. She mainly tried to stay out of his way. In her own way she grew to hate wanting his love and not being able to get it. She hated that part of herself that kept wanting his love or even just his approval long after she could see that he was never, never going to give it.

Out of nowhere he comes home from work angry. He reaches the porch yelling and screaming at the woman inside—yelling that she is his wife, he can do with her what he wants. They do not understand what is happening. He is pushing, hitting, telling her to shut up. She is pleading—crying. He does not want to hear, to listen. They catch his angry words in their hands like lightning bugs—store them in a jar to sort them out later. Words about other men, about phone calls, about how he had told her. They do not know what he has told her. They have never heard them talk in an angry way.

She thinks of all the nights she lies awake in her bed hearing the woman's voice, her mother's voice, hearing his voice. She wonders if it is then that he is telling her everything—warning her. Yelling, screaming, hitting: they stare at the red blood that trickles through the crying mouth. They cannot believe this pleading, crying woman, this woman who does not fight back, is the same person they know. The person they know is strong, gets things done, is a woman of ways and means, a woman of action. They do not know her still, paralyzed, waiting for the next blow, pleading. They do not know their mama afraid. Even if she does not hit back they want her to run, to run and to not stop running. She wants her to hit him with the table light, the ashtray, the one near her hand. She does not want to see her like this, not fighting back. He notices them, long enough to tell them to get out, go upstairs. She refuses to move. She cannot move. She cannot leave her mama alone. When he says What are you staring at, do you want some, too? she is afraid enough to move. She will not take her orders from him. She asks the woman if it is right to leave her alone. The woman—her mother—nods her head yes. She still stands still. It is his movement in her direction that sends her up the stairs. She cannot believe all her sisters and her brother are not taking a stand, that they go to sleep. She cannot bear their betrayal. When the father is not looking she creeps down the steps. She wants the woman to know that she is not alone. She wants to bear witness.

50

ALL THAT SHE does not understand about marriage, about men and women, is explained to her one night. In her dark place on the stairs she is seeing over and over again the still body of the woman pleading, crying, the moving body of the man angry, yelling. She sees that the man has a gun. She hears him tell the woman that he will kill her. She sits in her place on the stair and demands to know of herself is she able to come to the rescue, is she willing to fight, is she ready to die. Her body shakes with the answers. She is fighting back the tears. When he leaves the room she comes to ask the woman if she is all right, if there is anything she can do. The woman's voice is full of tenderness and hurt. She is in her role as mother. She tells her daughter to go upstairs and go to sleep, that everything will be all right. The daughter does not believe her. Her eyes are pleading. She does not want to be told to go. She hovers in the shadows. When he returns he tells her that he has told her to get her ass upstairs. She does not look at him. He turns to the woman, tells her to leave, tells her to take the daughter with her.

The woman does not protest. She moves like a robot, hurriedly throwing things into suitcases, boxes. She says nothing to the man. He is still screaming, muttering. When she tries to say to him he is wrong, so wrong, he is more angry, threatening. All the neat drawers are emptied out on the bed, all the precious belongings that can be carried, stuffed, are to be taken. There is sorrow in every gesture, sorrow and pain—like a dust collecting on everything, so thick she can gather it in her hands. She is seeing that the man owns everything, that the woman has only her clothes, her shoes, and other personal belongings. She is seeing that the woman can be told to go, can be sent away in the silent, long hours of the night. She is hearing in her head the man's threats to kill. She can feel the cool metal as if it is resting against her cheek. She can hear the click, the blast. She can see the woman's body falling. No, it is not her body, it is the body of love. She witnesses the death of love. If love were alive she believes it would stop everything. It would steady the man's voice, calm his rage. Love would take the woman's hand, caress her cheek and with a clean handkerchief wipe her eyes. The gun is pointed at love. He lays it on the table. He wants his wife to finish her packing, to go.

She is again in her role as mother. She tells the daughter that she does not have to flee in the middle of the night, that it is not her fight. The daughter is silent, staring into the woman's eyes. She is looking for the bright lights, the care and adoration she has shown the man. The eyes are dark with grief, swollen. She feels that a fire inside the woman is dying out, that she is cold. She is sure the woman will freeze to death if she goes out into the night alone. She takes her hand, ready to go with her. Yet she hopes there will be no going. She hopes when the mother's brother comes he will be strong enough to take love's body and give it, mouth-to-mouth, the life it has lost. She hopes he will talk to the man, guide him. When he finally comes, her mother's favorite brother, she cannot believe the calm way he lifts suitcase, box, sack, carries them to the car without question. She cannot bear his silent agreement that the man is right, that he has done what men are able to do. She cannot take the bits and pieces of her mother's heart and put them together again.

51

I AM ALWAYS fighting with mama. Everything has come between us. She no longer stands between me and all that would hurt me. She is hurting me. This is my dream of her—that she will stand between me and all that hurts me, that she will protect me at all cost. It is only a dream. In some way I understand that it has to do with marriage, that to be the wife to the husband she must be willing to sacrifice even her daughters for his good. For the mother it is not simple. She is always torn. She works hard to fulfill his needs, our needs. When they are not the same she must maneuver, manipulate, choose. She has chosen. She has decided in his favor. She is a religious woman. She has been told that a man should obey god, that a woman should obey man, that children should obey their fathers and mothers, particularly their mothers. I will not obey.

She says that she punishes me for my own good. I do not know what it is I have done this time. I know that she is ready with her switches, that I am to stand still while she lashes out again and again. In my mind there is the memory of a woman sitting still while she is being hit, punished. In my mind I am remembering how much I want that woman to fight back. Before I can think clearly my hands reach out, grab the switches, are raised as if to hit her back. For a moment she is stunned, unbelieving. She is shocked. She tells me that I must never *ever* as long as I live raise my hand against my mother. I tell her I do not have a mother. She is even more shocked. Enraged, she lashes out again. This time I am still. This time I cry. I see the hurt in her eyes when I say I do not have a mother. I am ready to be punished. My desire was to stop the pain, not to hurt. I am ashamed and torn. I do not want to stand still and be punished but I never want to hurt mama. It is better to hurt than to cause her pain. She warns me that she will tell daddy when he comes home, that I will be punished again. I cannot understand her acts of betrayal. I cannot understand that she must be against me to be for him. He and I are strangers. Deep in the night we parted from one another, knowing that nothing would ever be the same. He did not say good-bye. I did not look him in the face. Now we avoid one another. He speaks to me through her.

Although they act as if everything between them is the same, that life is as it was. It is only a game. They pretend. There is no pain in the pretense. Everything is hidden.

Secrets find a way out in sleep. My sisters say to mama She cries in her sleep, calls out. In her sleep is the place of remembering. It is the place where there is no pretense. She is dreaming always the same dream. A movie is showing. It is a tragic story of jealousy and lost love. It is called *Crime of Passion.* In the movie a man has killed his wife and daughter. He has killed his wife because he believes she has lovers. He has killed the daughter because she witnesses the death of the wife. When they go to trial all the remaining family come to speak on behalf of the man. At his job he is calm and quiet, a hardworking man, a family man. Neighbors come to testify that the dead woman was young and restless, that the daughter was wild and rebellious. Everyone sympathizes with the man. His story is so sad that they begin to weep. All their handkerchiefs are clean and white. Like flags waving, they are a signal of peace, of surrender. They are a gesture to the man that he can go on with life.

52

WE CANNOT BELIEVE we must leave our beloved Crispus Attucks and go to schools in the white neighborhoods. We cannot imagine what it will be like to walk by the principal's office and see a man who will not know our name, who will not care about us. Already the grown-ups are saying it will be nothing but trouble, but they do not protest. Already we feel like the cattle in the stockyard near our house, herded, prodded, pushed. Already we prepare ourselves to go willingly to what will be a kind of slaughter, for parts of ourselves must be severed to make this integration of schools work. We start by leaving behind the pleasure we will feel in going to our all-black school, in seeing friends, in being a part of a school community. Our pleasure is replaced by fear. We must rise early to catch the buses that will take us to the white schools. So early that we must go into the gymnasium and wait for the other students, the white students, to arrive. Again we are herded, prodded, pushed, told not to make trouble in this early morning waiting period.

Sometimes there is protest. Everyone black walks out, except for those whose parents have warned that there will be no walking out of school. I do not walk out. I do not believe that any demands made will be met. We surrendered the right to demand when the windows to Attucks were covered with wood and barred shut, when the doors were locked. Anyhow, mama has warned us about walking out. The walkouts make everything worse. More than ever before we are cattle, to be herded, prodded, pushed. More than ever before we are slaughtered. We can hear the sound of the paddles reverberating in the hallway as black boys are struck by the white principals. The word spreads rapidly when one of us has been sent home not knowing when and if they will be allowed to come back.

Some of us are chosen. We are allowed to sit in the classes with white students. We are told that we are smart. We are the good servants who will be looked to. We are to stand between the white administration and the black student body. We are not surprised that black boys are not in the smart classes, even though we know that many of them are smart. We know that white folks have this thing about black boys sitting in classes with white girls. Now and then a smart black boy is moved into the classes. They have been watching him. He has proved himself. We know that we are all being watched, that we must prove ourselves. We no longer like attending school. We are tired of the long hours spent discussing what can be done to make integration work. We discuss with them knowing all the while that they want us to do something, to change, to make ourselves into carbon copies of them so that they can forget we are here, so that they can forget the injustice of their past. They are not prepared to change.

Although black and white attend the same school, blacks sit with blacks and whites with whites. In the cafeteria there is no racial mixing. When hands reach out to touch across these boundaries whites protest, blacks protest as well. Each one seeing it as a going over to the other side. School is a place where we came face to face with racism. When we walk through the rows of national guardsmen with their uniforms and guns we think that we will be the first to die, to lay our bodies down. We feel despair and long for the days when school was a place where we learned to love and celebrate ourselves, a place where we were number one.

53

THEY ARE CONCERNED because she has not shown the right interest in boys. They do not talk to her about what it is about boys that she finds boring, uninteresting. She cannot talk to them. She cannot tell them how much she hates anyone to lord it over her. She cannot tell them that this is what boys often want to do. She cannot explain that she does not like to be touched, grabbed at, without agreeing to such touching. She is disgusted by the grabbing, the pleading that she let them do this and do that. Even when she is aroused, the feeling goes away when boys behave as though there is only something in this moment for them, something they are seeking that she must give. She is not ashamed to say no. She does not care that the word gets around that she will say no. She cares that she is left alone. She has no date for the senior prom. Her would-be date, someone she is talking to from out of town, someone who drives a sports car, who has a job working for a newspaper, says he will come when she asks him, then changes his mind without saying why. They will not let her go with that theater crowd she hangs out with, that group of rather wild white teenagers. They are concerned that she may be growing up funny. They watch her behavior. They think about the way a certain funny grown-up woman showed intense interest in her. They think that maybe they were wrong to allow her to accept presents, a dress, a watch with tiny diamonds. They are sure that she is not showing enough willingness to seek out boys and do what girls do. They are watching.

Every now and then they agree that she can visit with a girlfriend who lives across town, who is white, who drives a convertible. They listen to their phone conversations to hear what is being discussed, books, politics, boys. They hear that she is mainly listening to the white girl talking about the boys that interest her. They do not know that she is interested in young men but does not talk about them because they are not anybody the white girl knows. When her friend drives her home from school they sit outside and talk, sometimes for hours. They tell her this cannot happen, that she must come inside and let that white girl go home.

She does not tell them when the white girl tries to kill herself. They are just glad that she no longer comes around. She never tells anyone at home about the scars on her friend's wrists. She never tells that she and her white friend share a feeling of being outside, alone, that they comfort one another. She knows that they will think it silly, downright crazy, to want to die because some boy does not love you, does not notice even that you are alive. She understands. She takes her friend's hand. They embrace one another in the stillness of the car. They share the promise that the friend will never again act without talking about it first. They hold each other close, glad to be alive, glad to be friends.

When she enters the door her mother and father say nothing, even though they have been watching. Later in the night they keep her downstairs and want to know what is going on between her and the friend. She tells them they are friends, nothing is going on. Her daddy says, Don't lie to me. She looks at him with anger and contempt. She has no answers for them. They tell her that they will have none of this in their house, that she will have to go. She is not sure why they are so upset. She does not understand. Shaken by the fear of being told to leave, by threats of punishment, she agrees to stop seeing her friend. She does not understand why they want to take this friend from her. She does not know that they are worried that she may grow funny.

54

THEY ARE RELIEVED that she is finally showing an interest in boys, but even that is something she does not do right. She likes a boy who is younger than herself—that is simply not done. They do not complain because they are so relieved. They laugh about it. They are glad at least that he is taller than she is, that he does not look younger. She likes him because he does not lord it over her, because he is always in a good mood. With him she is never afraid. It is not because he is younger, it is because of the way he is. He does not plead with her to give him some. They are content to touch each other, to explore. She likes to feel the wetness inside his pants. Now that she is interested in boys they are warning her not to become pregnant, not to bring any children into that house. She knows how to say no. She knows how to avoid getting to the place where no is hard to say. When she breaks up with him it is because he is someone she cannot talk to about the things that really matter. He is only concerned with basketball. She likes basketball and watching basketball players. She likes to see their bodies move. They remind her of deer, of tender fawns moving gracefully through the woods. She is interested in books and the grace of basketball, in ideas.

Another older basketball player interests her. He attracts her eyes because he has skin that is a satin silklike black. Dark enough to make the whites of his eyes look as if they are hiding, shielding themselves from the too much beauty he exudes. She lusts after him. And she is not the only one. Daring in her passion, she calls him to let him know. He is interested. She is one of the good girls, the smart girls, one of the ones that will go to college. He knows that she will not give him any. He does not care. He knows where to go when he wants to get sex. No one ever talks to him about ideas, life, and desire at the same time. Her desire is curious and strong. Like homemade whiskey, it warms him quickly. Several times he tries to move close to her. Yet he knows she is not for him. His own mother has warned him. He has seen the stone-cold look on her father's face.

He cannot believe she is not afraid. She slips into the backseat of his car. He wants to show her that she should be afraid, that she is not for him. She does not sit in front with him, choosing the back. Her voice moves seductively in the night, caressing his ears with the tenderness of her words. She feels safe with him without knowing why. He stops the car out in the country on a deserted road. She wants to know if this is where he brings girls on weekends after the basketball games. He does not answer. He moves into the backseat as if he is entering a cage, a trap in which he and not she will be imprisoned. He feels her innocence is too much. She is beginning to feel afraid, afraid because she is innocent. He has never let innocence stand in his way. It is her trust that catches him. He is not to be trusted. Perhaps he, too, has heard the words A black nigger is a no-good nigger. He wants to be trusted. His cold hands around her neck do not make her afraid. He says no to her caresses and kisses. He says no, the night is fleeting—it is late—he must take her home.

55

BLACK WOMEN DO not go with white men. They learn early that all a white man does to a black woman is ruin her, prostitute her, throw her away like an old rag. There is a white man driving around naked in their neighborhood. No one calls the police. They know nothing will be done. In black neighborhoods white men can do as they please. They are told not to go over to the cars of white men who stop them on the street, to look straight ahead, to keep on walking. They are afraid to walk down one street. Like a bridge it connects the black neighborhood to the places where white folks live. There are no houses on this street, only warehouses—loosening floors. There the white men are most likely to drive by and yell out. Even as they look straight ahead, keep on walking, they feel afraid. Somehow they have learned without knowing why that nothing much stands between to protect them from the harm white men want to do to them. When white men come to the door and no grown person is home they know not to let them in. They know not to be fooled by the business suits, the briefcases. They know that the smiles are poison, not to touch the outstretched hands. They know to say nothing when he says Cat got your tongue.

When they go to the integrated schools they learn that all white men are suspect, not just the ones in cars on the street, not just the ones lurking in black neighborhoods. They must watch out for the ones who are teachers, principals. They must suspect all friendly gestures. They say white boys are never cute. They do not talk to white boys if they can avoid it, even though they are not afraid of the white boys in their class.

There is a white boy that she likes. They work together on the yearbook. They work together on the senior play. They become friends. She does not think ever of him as a boyfriend. She knows better. Anyway he reminds her of a lizard. Her mother says to be friends at school is fine but he cannot come to their house. She is shocked to find that racial barriers exist in her house, disappointed, ashamed. Her parents are afraid that this friendship is too close. They want to see it end before anyone gets the wrong ideas. Even so, when his parents, respected in the community, call to see if she can come to their house for dinner, they agree. He comes for her in the gray car that she admires and secretly loves. He loves the car, too. They take the long way to his house.

She can see that he has demanded that his parents prove they are not racist with actions, not just with words. She admires his parents, that they love him enough to act. She tells him later that she will not be this little experiment he uses to test his parents. Alone in his room, listening to records, she says no to his kiss. She says no she will not be used to test his parents' love. They are friends. He is not surprised that she can see through him. He tells her that it is not that he does not want her to be a girlfriend but that he can see that she is not interested. She tells him that she cannot be interested when it seems that she is only a way for him to announce his own rebellion. They take the long way home. A carload of white men seeing a black girl and a white boy together try to run them off the road.

56

THEY SAY SHE is too skinny. They cannot stand the way she looks. They say she looks like one of those pictures of starving children, the ones in magazines where their eyes are pleading for help. They do not say whether or not her eyes are pleading. She looks at her eyes in the mirror and sees that they are red with crying, red with the fear of being too skinny, ugly, unwanted. Her brother loves to tell the story about how the wind blows her off the front porch and he has to run to catch up with her. They know it is only a story that he has made up but they laugh so hard he tells it again and again. She looks at him with hate. His teasing is a betrayal of all the pleasures they once shared. Growing up divides them. He is ashamed to love a girl. He must show in every way that there is nothing about her that he can stand. He must not be on the side of the outcast. He tells her that she is too skinny to ever have a boyfriend. She does not have the hips and legs that boys like. He tells her that if she is not careful she will have an ironing board butt, one that is so flat, flatter than a pancake.

They buy her pills to help her gain weight. They make her drink a raw egg in a glass of milk daily. They give her vitamins and tonics. They want to see meat on her bones. They warn her that if she gets sick she will probably die from losing so much weight. She does not care about gaining weight. She does not care about the way she looks. She wants to do whatever she can to make them stop the teasing, to make them happy. They buy clothes for her that are sizes too big. They think the clothes will make her grow. They need to pretend that she is not so thin. The clothes hang on her like wet clothes on a line, shapeless and without dignity. They say her arms and legs are like toothpicks. She never wears shorts in summer. She never wears blouses without sleeves that show her arms. They tell her that she looks like Saru, old and frail. She does not tell them that she is proud to look like Saru, like a reed in the wind. They tell her she looks more like her every day.

She has difficulty eating. Long after everyone has left the kitchen she stares into the cold food on her plate. They have warned her that if it is not all finished and soon she will be whipped. Her tears make the cold food stick in her throat. She runs to the bathroom choking. She is whipped. Each night they wait to see if she has eaten all the food on her plate. They watch her movements as if she were an animal in the circus. They say she eats like a bird, picking at her food bit by bit. They yell at her to stop eating that way, to stop playing with the food. She does not know why it is she cannot eat. She wants not to sit alone in the cold kitchen watching the tears form puddles in her plate. When they are not watching she looks for places to hide the food. She throws each white bean behind the refrigerator, behind the stove. Sometimes they tell. Then she has to clean up the food and is given more to eat. She must sit and eat even if it takes all night.

In the cold kitchen, staring out the window, she thinks about Wordsworth and Shelley, about Dickinson, Whitman and Frost. She thinks about ways to escape punishment. Every now and then, if the food is still hot, someone will help her eat it because they feel sorry, because they cannot stand to see her sitting alone crying. If they are caught she will be punished. She knows that no matter what they do she will not get bigger. They cannot give up trying. They believe they are saving her life.

57

I HAVE DISCOVERED paint. Mixing the water with the powder makes color bright and primary. I imagine that I have returned to the cave of my childhood dreams, to the paintings on the wall. The art teacher, Mr. Harold, watches me stirring. He tells me he has been watching me since class began, that he enjoys the sight of a student falling in love with color again and again. He brings me a stack of paper. I wait always before I begin painting. He says I take too long, that such intense concentration may block the creativity. I want him to leave me alone. I am silent. He understands. He will come back later. I am trying to remember the pictures in the cave, the animals. If I can paint them all I am sure I can discover again the secret of living, what it was I left in the cave. I start with the color black. In a book on the history of pigments I come across a new phrase, *bone black*. Bone black is a black carbonaceous substance obtained by calcifying bones in closed vessels. Burning bones, that's what it makes me think about—flesh on fire, turning black, turning into ash.

Mr. Harold laughs when I tell him that all my life I have heard my mother say black is a woman's color—a color denied me because I am a child. He wears black pants and black shirts with funny ties. He can look this way because he is the art teacher, because he is an artist. In this integrated high school he is one of the few white teachers who does not keep black kids at arm's length, who is not afraid. He cares. He is the only one who seems to understand that the whites and their hatreds are the problem and not us. He does not deny us. He does not deny me the color black. He urges me to stay with it but to add color, to do more with it.

I begin with the mouth of the cave, add red to the black. The red is the heart of the seekers, the animals and human beings who come. The next picture is one of the fire. Up close, with outstretched hands feeling the warmth, I remember that the fire is not just the color red, that it is blue and yellow and green. These are the colors of the lost spirits. Mixed together they bring new life to color. At the bottom of the fire is the color black. This is the ash that the fire becomes. This is the remains of all the animals who have given their life in sacrifice to keep the spirit moving, burning bright. I want to make the color gray, to paint a world covered in mist, but this painting must wait, for it is what I see when I leave the cave. The animals must be painted. I try and try but cannot get them right. Mr. Harold looks at me from his desk and says no as he sees me about to rip the paper, to throw it away. He shakes his head, no. He has told me many times to keep at it, to look at it, to rethink what it is I am trying to do. Without remembering all the animals I leave watercolor behind; I am on to acrylic, to painting on canvas.

The color black is sometimes harsh. I abandon it now and then for the colors red, yellow, and brown. The picture I am painting is of the wilderness my spirit roams in. I tell him that I left the cave and went into the wilderness. He tells me to let the color show what the wilderness is like. All around are fading colors that contain bits of pieces of their earlier brightness. I call this painting *Autumn in the Wilderness.*

58

SLOWLY I HAVE become involved in campus ministry. Leaders in the crusade for christ in our town do radical political work as well for they dare to cross the barriers between white and black. They hold integrated meetings. They embrace everyone. They live the meaning that we are all one. I have become involved slowly because my faith is not as strong as theirs. I am not strongly enough a believer in sin. In fact I do not believe in it at all, evil yes but sin no. And god, I am a true true believer in all gods.

To cure my asthma they have a laying on of hands. It is a hot summer night. We are all together on a farm outside town listening to the crickets. We are all kneeling. Everyone whose hand can reach touches me or something of mine. Although my breathing continues to move in and out in a painful way those hands are blessing me, holding me in a sweeter love than that we experience one to one. They pray that god's love, which is all expansive, will take us all in, will heal us all, but especially will heal the asthma. I do not believe in cause and effect. My asthma attacks continue. It is not a lack of faith. I believe in the power of the hands. I believe in the miraculous. And the miracle will come later. Though I have long lost touch with the many hands, it is the power of that night that makes all other nights of healing possible.

To strengthen our ties with one another we go to a retreat. It is only after the white grown-ups, respected in the community, have called to plead my cause for me that mama allows me to go. She restricts my movements constantly for fear that these new experiences are ruining me, making me disconsolate. This is the new word they use to describe me. I give it to them. I learn it at church when we are singing Come ye disconsolate wherever ye languish, come to the mercy fervently kneel, here bring your wounded heart, hear tell your anguish, earth has no sorrow that heaven cannot heal. I am not crazy, I tell them. I am disconsolate. I show them in the dictionary that it means dejected, deprived of consolation. Whatever it is, they are sick of it. They are waiting for it to go away. They do not understand that I am also waiting for it to go away.

Here among the faithful I can reveal that I am anguished in spirit. They understand the primacy of the spirit. When we sing together, eat, and join hands I feel there is solace, that this is a mercy seat where I can rest. The group is led by the energy of a middle-aged white woman. She and I take a walk together to get more in touch with one another. We talk about the healing power of love. I want to take the sincerity of our talk, our faith, and cover the world with it like icing on a cake. I want to understand why the healing does not spread outward. I want to know why if the healing is real it does not touch us in the places where we live. At home they are concerned about this new passion for the group, for god. They want to make sure that the god that is talked about, worshiped and prayed to, is the god of the old and new testament and not the god of this rewritten paperback Bible.

59

TO US THE Catholic church is a mystery. We know there
is strong prejudice against Catholics among the white folks
in this town. Black folks say religion is all the same. The
Catholic church is one of the few white churches black
people have joined with no protest. Black folks say the few
that join do so just for show. We children come to believe
that the one difference between the Catholic church and
our Baptist church is the degree of show. Catholicism is
more showy—with the robes, the candles, and all that
singing and praying in a language most people cannot
understand. We go there only once for an interfaith Christmas service. We are impressed by the show even though
we do not feel moved in spirit, we do not feel the hand of
god pressing against our heart when the priest speaks.
We are fascinated by the idea of confession, especially me.

We want to ask the Catholics at school what confession is like but we don't because we know better.

When I become active in the campus crusade for christ, I meet and talk to Catholics for the first time. We attend a retreat where believers come from all around to join together. Banners on every wall say The Way Is One But The Paths Are Many. We are Methodist, Baptist, Lutheran, Catholic, Episcopalian. There are only a few of us who are not white. We retreat to a place in the hills. It is early spring and everywhere flowers bloom. There is a glory everywhere in nature that seems to echo the exuberance in the voice of the true believers, the true crusaders. I am still filled with doubt. I am glad to be at the retreat, to escape the tensions of home, the feeling that I stand on the edge of a cliff about to fall off. I know that many people come to god to be rescued, to be taken from the cliff and placed on solid ground. I come to god and yet remain at the edge of the cliff. I have not been rescued. For comfort I read over and over the story of John the Baptist wandering in the wilderness. I too linger in the wilderness wanting desperately to find my way.

We are to hear a talk from the Catholic priest who is here. It is the opening session of the retreat. He is wearing clothes that are a slate gray, dark but not black. It is hard for me to imagine him wearing black, since I have been told all my life that black is a woman's color. He is lean and without the plump smug flesh that so often identifies the men called by god. When he speaks I feel as though we have suddenly entered a room where only he and I are present. This feeling disturbs me. I look around me to make sure that everyone else is still there. They are staring straight ahead. They, too, have entered that room. With me his voice is soft-spoken, gentle. He tells me that he understands the aloneness that I feel, that he sees me poised on the edge of a cliff.

For the first time in my life I hear someone say that there is nothing wrong with feeling alone, that he, too, has been at the edge, has felt the fear of drowning, of being moved toward death without consciously contemplating suicide. I do not ask him how he knows, how he feels with me this pain in my heart. When the talk ends, when we are alone, he repeats again and again the words that are a net catching the body falling from a tall place. When I weep and sob all over the slate gray clothing he tells me that the young woman standing on the cliff, alone and afraid to live, is only suspended in a moment of hesitation, that she will overcome her fear and leap into life—that she will bring with her the treasures that are her being: the beauty, the courage, the wisdom. He tells me to let that young woman into my heart, to begin to love her so that she can live and live and go on living.

60

CLOTHES DO NOT interest her. They hang on her body as if they are there only because there is no place else for them to go, like men on street corners, like children on the school playground on weekends. Her clothes are always chosen by someone else. She never likes them. She puts together outfits that do not match, socks that are not the same color. She does not think that any clothes can look nice on a body that is so skinny. She wants to forget that this is her body. They want her to remember. They want her to pay more attention to what she is wearing. They say she looks old. They buy her clothes to make her look young, baby pinks, sky blue, sunflower yellow. She cannot stand the thought of wearing yet another pink dress, she cannot stand the thought of ruffles and puffed sleeves. She is happy when the latest style is pleated skirts and white blouses. She likes reds, dark greens, and only a certain color yellow. She likes colors that remind her of autumn, of falling leaves and barren branches, of fire burning.

They say she cannot wear the color red because it is too old for a young girl, that maybe she will be ready when she is near the end of high school. She knows that red is the color of passion, that a woman in a red dress is sultry, sensuous, that a woman wearing a red dress had better look out. Red is a color for sluts and whores they say. She is trying on yet another pink dress. They say She looks so innocent, so sweet in the color pink. Secretly she loves the color black. It is the color of night and hidden passion. When the women go dancing, when they dress up to go to the nightclub they wear black slips. They sit in front of the mirror painting themselves with makeup, making their lips red and rich. To her they are more beautiful in their black slips than they will ever be in any dress. She cannot wait to wear one. For now she would be content to wear a black skirt. When she tells her mother that she loves the color black, that she wants to wear a black dress, she is told black is a woman's color. In her dreams all wonderful things denied are the color black. She wants to wear a black skirt with a white blouse so she becomes an usher at church. She can only wear the black skirt one Sunday in every month. She can never wear it to school.

When they go to buy winter coats, she picks out two. One a deep dark red, the other her favorite black. She cannot have the black coat. Her mama does not want to say again Black is a woman's color. She should know that by now. She should know better. She cannot put the black coat back on the hanger without first pressing it close to her cheek, holding it the way you hold all things you must love and lose. She cannot have the red coat either. They say it makes her look too grown-up. She must choose between sky blue and pea green. She hates light blue. It is the color of all cold and heartless things. She suggests a navy blue coat, one that will not get dirty fast, one that will go with everything. They think that this is not a bad idea. She is nearly happy—navy blue so close to her beloved black.

When she is older she will wear black every day. She wants to know how soon it will be, how soon will she be able to wear a black dress. They say never if you do not shut up talking about it. She cannot wait to be a woman. She cannot wait to wear the color black. She is looking in the mirror, playing pretend. She is a woman wearing a black dress. She is not in mourning. She has learned to put all the broken bits and pieces of her heart back together again. She is a woman. She is dressed in black. She has been told all her life Black is a woman's color.

61

LONELINESS BRINGS ME to the edge of what I know. My soul is dark like the inner world of the cave—bone black. I have been drowning in that blackness. Like quicksand it sucks me in and keeps me there in the space of all my pain. I never say out loud that I could die in this space of loneliness, of outsiderness. I never say out loud I want to kill myself—to go away from all this. I never tell anyone how much I want to belong. The priest I met saw me standing on the edge of a cliff about to jump off and pulled me back. It was not a real cliff, just the one inside myself. Before anyone goes to that real place where we leap to our death, the dying has to be imagined. And so he finds me there in that bone black place within myself where I am dreaming my escape.

He sends a student to spend time with me at the retreat. She gives me Rilke's *Letters to a Young Poet*. I am drowning and his words come to rescue me. He helps to make sense of the pain I feel. Now it is Rilke who speaks to me and urges me to go into myself and find the deeps into which my life takes rise. At last I am not alone. I have been seen.

I read poems. I write. That is my destiny. Standing on the edge of the cliff about to fall into the abyss, I remember who I am. I am a young poet, a writer. I am here to make words. I have the power to pull myself back from death—to keep myself alive.

Now when they tell me I am crazy, that if I keep reading all those books I will end up crazy, locked away in the asylum where no one will visit me—now when they tell me this I am not so afraid. Rilke gives meaning to the wilderness of spirit I am living in. His book is a world I enter and find myself. He tells me that everything terrible is really something helpless that wants help from us. I read *Letters to a Young Poet* over and over. I am drowning and it is the raft that takes me safely to the shore.

Now when I lie in bed at night thinking that it is better to die than always to be misunderstood, always to feel so much pain, I know that I am not alone. Lying in the dark I repeat the words, "Do not believe that he who would seek to comfort you lives untroubled." I still suffer. Daddy Gus says that my suffering will end. That one day I will look back on all of this and it will not matter.

I take my book to read him passages. Like Rilke, he tells me not to be afraid to look deep into everything, not to be afraid even of the pain. I can tell him, my grandfather who loves me always, that I want to belong—that it hurts to be always on the outside. He tells me there are lots of ways to belong in this world. And that it is my work to find out where I belong.

At night when everyone is silent and everything is still, I lie in the darkness of my windowless room, the place where they exile me from the community of their heart, and search the unmoving blackness to see if I can find my way home. I tell myself stories, write poems, record my dreams. In my journal I write—I belong in this place of words. This is my home. This dark, bone black inner cave where I am making a world for myself.

About the Author

bell hooks is Distinguished Professor of English at City College in New York City, where she makes her home.

From one
SEXY Bee-atch...
To another :-) !
you guys are a
Blast...
see you in the
BIG TIME!

Julie Allson